AN ESSAY ON LANGUAGE

ROBERT A. HALL, JR.
Cornell University

AN ESSAY ON LANGUAGE

CHILTON BOOKS / EDUCATIONAL DIVISION
Publishers

PHILADELPHIA   NEW YORK

2095

Designed by Rafael Millán

MANUFACTURED IN THE UNITED STATES OF AMERICA
BY QUINN & BODEN COMPANY, INC., RAHWAY, N. J.

To
Hans Kurath

HAROLD K. HARVEY
CHURCHILL FALLS SCHOOL
CHURCHILL FALLS
LABRADOR W., NEWFOUNDLAND

PREFACE

This monograph, with the somewhat eighteenth-century title *An Essay on Language*, represents essentially a *prise de position* on my part with regard to certain of the central questions in current debates over the nature of human linguistic systems and our techniques of analyzing and describing them. To a certain extent, also, it is an explication of the theoretical bases implicit, but perhaps not always sufficiently explicit, in certain recent works of mine (especially *Idealism in Romance Linguistics*, 1963; *Introductory Linguistics*, 1964; *Pidgin and Creole Languages*, 1966) which have not always been rightly understood—especially with regard to the applicability of scientific method in linguistic study. Since I am concerned with theories, not personalities, no living scholars are mentioned by name (except in the brief final Bibliography) or quoted directly, even where (as in a number of instances) others have phrased one point or another more felicitously than I could ever hope to do.

It is presumed that the reader is already acquainted, to a certain extent, with the issues being debated in linguistics in the 1960's. Nevertheless, since a number of the terms occurring in my discussion have been used with widely different meanings, a short glossary is appended so as to give the senses in which I use them here.

No discussion of the problems treated here could ever hope to be permanent or definitive, and no such claim is made for this essay. If it helps in any way to re-introduce at least a modicum of objectivity and clarity into the discussion of current issues in linguistics, I shall consider that my efforts have not been wholly in vain.

R. A. H., Jr.

Ithaca, N. Y., May 1968.

TABLE OF CONTENTS

AN ESSAY ON LANGUAGE

1

NON-LINGUISTIC PREMISES

The use of language is, as we all recognize, one of the major characteristics (if not, indeed, *the* major characteristic) distinguishing humans from other living beings. As a result, our interest in language, as an exclusively human phenomenon, is extensive and long-lasting. Presumably, discussion of language and its characteristics began as soon as men started to reflect on their own nature. Over the centuries, the analysis and formulation of human linguistic activities has closely followed current fashions in speculative thought: classical philosophy in Graeco-Roman times, scholastic argumentation in the Middle Ages, rationalism in the seventeenth and eighteenth centuries, and scientific method in the nineteenth and twentieth. It is of course dangerous to use any system of symbols for discussion and description of the system itself, because in so doing we run the risk of arguing in a circle, i.e. allowing our conclusions about the system to be influenced by the nature of the very system in which our analysis is framed. It is customary, in this connection, to cite Franz Mauthner's wise-crack, that talking about language is like building a fire in a wooden stove. Nevertheless, discussion of language has continued and, in recent decades, with the extensive development of linguistics, greatly increased.

A major part of the debates over linguistic theory in the twentieth century has been concerned with the status of linguistics as a science. On both sides of the Atlantic, since the end of the eighteenth century, a host of workers in philology and linguistics have concerned themselves with developing methods of observing human linguistic activities, analyzing them, and formulating the relationship between their various aspects, that might be as scientific as possible. These efforts have not gone un-opposed. Other philologists and linguists, as well as workers in non-linguistic fields (such as philosophy and psychology), have denied either the possibility of applying scientific methods to the study of language, or the scientific nature of work that has been done by those with whose out-look on language they disagree. In some quarters, it has become the fashion to sneer at any at-tempt to render linguistics objective and impersonal as "naïve scientism". As a result, the entire question as to whether lin-guistics can or should be treated as a science is still, unfortunately, a matter of debate. My purpose here is to take up once again the entire problem of human language and its amenability to scientific study, especially certain recent developments in gen-eral linguistic theory.

Before discussing language itself, however, it will be nec-essary to make explicit certain fundamental premises concerning various non-linguistic aspects of our subject, which are often implicit and hence go unrecognized in our discussions: the nature of scientific inquiry, the relation between individual and society, the place of different types of analysis in the study of human activity, and the time-factor in our observation of the world around us. If this is not done, we run the risk of extensive and serious misunderstanding of such underlying notions as "science," "collectivity," or the frequently cited opposition between "syn-chronic" and "diachronic." The study of language does not form an inherent part of these aspects of our knowledge, but they form a back-ground against which and in relation to which our discus-sion must take place.

We must first clarify the issue of the applicability of a scientific approach to linguistics. There has been extensive discussion of the nature of scientific inquiry, but much of what has often been considered essential to science (e.g. laboratory-technique) is not applicable to a great part of human activity. Yet a scientific approach always includes certain essential features whose applicability to the study of human patterns of living has been amply demonstrated. Above all, observation of facts, by the most effective means and techniques available, must take priority over any other type of study. On the basis of facts attested in this way, we can form abstractions, i.e. set up analytical entities resulting from and subsuming our observation of features common to two or more phenomena. Thus, in phonology, a single actual sound, or a number of sounds, are facts, primary data; a sound-type (e.g. "bilabial voiced plosive contoid," "high-front lip-rounded vocoid," etc.) is an abstraction, as is also a phoneme subsuming one or more sound-types. Much scientific work deals with abstractions rather than with directly observed facts; but facts must determine abstractions, not vice-versa, and whatever theory we build up must have facts (or abstractions based thereon) as its basis. No theory which does not start from facts and remain ultimately anchored to facts—no matter how great a degree of abstraction it may reach—is worth anything in scientific analysis. Fictions—factors in an analysis which simply do not exist—can have a place in scientific method, but (as Hans Vaihinger pointed out many years ago) only on condition that their presence as fictions be recognized, and that their effect on the resultant analysis be removed before the definitive formulation of the end-product.

Needless to say, new facts are always coming to light, and new tools and techniques of observation and recording of evidence are constantly being developed, bringing new data, opening up new fields of inquiry, and casting new light on already existing knowledge. Hence no finding made according to scientific principles can ever be considered definitive. This is the basis for the often quoted and often misunderstood observation that "a scientific statement is one which is susceptible of disproof" (if,

[3]

of course, the necessary contrary evidence can be adduced). Persons who still think of science (as did, say, Taine or Zola) as a substitute for revealed religion, without the supernatural but still preserving an element of dogmatism and absolute truth, often express surprise or mockery on hearing this definition of a scientific statement. Such persons do not realize that, since our knowledge of the universe around us is fragmentary (and, in any foreseeable future, doomed to remain so) but constantly increasing, our formulations of this knowledge, as summed up in scientific statements, must always be provisory and subject to revision. Otherwise, they cease to be scientific and become theological.

Consequently, scientific research always proceeds on the basis of hypothesis and verification. In popular parlance, a hypothesis is often referred to as "mere," and thought to belong to an inferior order of formulation (as opposed to a permanent "truth"). On the contrary, the basic method of procedure in any scientific inquiry is to set up a hypothesis on the basis of observed data, and to test this hypothesis insofar as possible, especially by applying it to new evidence, or to already known facts to which it has not as yet been applied. In accordance with "Occam's razor" (*entia non sunt multiplicanda praeter necessitatem*), unnecessary hypotheses are to be avoided, and it is to be considered a progress when an unnecessary hypothesis is eliminated. If a hypothesis fits further data than those on which it was originally based, and furnishes an explanation for new data, it can be regarded as verified. No verification, however, is ever anything but tentative, no matter how far-reaching and universally applicable its results may seem to be. Further data may, at any time, serve to upset theories which may previously have seemed to be firmly and definitively established. Hence science knows no absolute "truths," but only hypotheses and their (always provisory) verification. To sneer at a hypothesis as "mere" and to reject it because it is "only" a hypothesis, is to show oneself ignorant of scientific method.

A consequence of these two basic characteristics of scientific method—objectivity and procedure by hypothesis and verification

[4]

—is that it must be impersonal. The findings of science depend, not (as do artistic creations) on the expression of character-traits peculiar to one individual alone, but on procedures which are, and must remain, independent of any one personality. (There is no room in linguistics, for example, for any-one to try to distinguish himself by flamboyant idiosyncrasies and to call himself "le poète de la linguistique.") Hence, unlike an artistic or a religious experience, a scientific experiment must be repeatable by any number of observers, and must give the same results provided the same material and tools of observation are used, and the same procedures are followed. Since his findings are, by their very nature, provisory (a characteristic which constitutes a merit, not a fault), the scientist is not haughty or arrogant, but humble, before the universe of which he is both a student and a part, and before whatever discoveries concerning it he may be able to make. Furthermore, science is cumulative. Each investigator builds on the findings of his predecessors, adding to them where possible, and where necessary correcting and reformulating them. However, if he has to rework preceding analyses or formulations, he does not do so out of any kind of *parti pris*, and does not misrepresent his predecessors' motives or attitudes. The *odium theologicum* or *esprit d'école* is inimical to a scientific approach; science knows no parties, factions, or "schools."

Certain negative characteristics of science emerge from the definition we have just given of it, as involving objectivity, procedure by hypothesis and verification, cumulativity, impersonality, and humility. Any type of apriorism—the imposition of a previously evolved theory upon facts without regard to its applicability, and the omission or distortion of facts in order to fit them into such a theory—is in itself obviously inimical to objective observation, and hence antiscientific. Especially one type of *a priori* approach, rationalism (particularly as developed in seventeenth- and eighteenth-century French thought), has no place in scientific work. This is particularly true in our study of language, since all "rational" arguments are ultimately derived (and re-

[5]

duced!) from the structure of language itself (usually, in our culture, from that of Latin, French, or English)—as when we are told that it is "rational" to assume that the "deep structure" of all languages must involve subject plus predicate, in that order. (This is the kind of argumentation Mauthner meant by "building a fire in a wooden stove.") No such thing as "reason" or "la raison" exists in the abstract, apart from the linguistic system on which it is based. A system which is only a reduction of a more extensive system can never serve as a valid instrument for analyzing the very system from which it is derived. (To paraphrase Pascal, *la langue a ses raisons que la raison ne connaît pas.*) It is, therefore, quite unscientific to reject the scientifically based findings of linguistics and cultural anthropology in favor of a return to an anti-scientific rationalism.

Another type of unscientific approach, which often gives rise to aprioristic analyses, is philosophical idealism—the view that facts do not have a real existence, but are simply the corporeal manifestation of an invisible, ungraspable "ideal," which is permanently inaccessible to direct observation or analysis but is somehow the only "reality." Such idealism, whether Platonic-monistic or Neo-Platonic-dualistic, can only be harmful to scientific inquiry. It furnishes its proponents an easy way for avoiding verification of any theory they may bring forth which is contrary to observed facts. We may regard scientific method as somewhat analogous to a conductor with high resistance to electric current, whereby light is produced; the idealistic approach is then like a conductor which offers the current a less resistant path, so that the current is "shorted" and no light is produced. This comparison was the basis for Leonard Bloomfield's oft-quoted remark that idealism and similar approaches "short-circuit inquiry." Another comparison might be with a "sanctuary" (as in aeroplane-warfare), a territory on which attacking planes are stationed and to which they can return without their pursuers being able to follow them to their home base —in the case of scientific inquiry, without the ideal "truth" being ever accessible to observation and verification. Neo-Platonism, in the Renaissance, gave rise to much beautiful literature (e.g. the dialogues of Pietro Bembo, or Joachim du Bellay's sonnet *L'Idée*), but literary beauty is no substitute for scientific method in the analysis of human activity, linguistic or non-linguistic.

"But abstractions," some-one may say, "surely abstractions exist, even if Platonic ideals don't." Of course they do—in fact, the making of abstractions is an essential part of the process of linguistic symbolization—but the question is, where? An abstraction is simply an ensemble of features characteristic of and common to two or more observed phenomena—for instance, the flat, round surface with a spiral groove having minute wavy variations in the wall and/or the bottom, which characterize a modern gramophone-record. This or any other abstraction does not exist in the real world; only the phenomena themselves have objective existence. Abstractions exist only inside the heads of the individuals who make them. Inevitably, therefore, my abstraction or "idea" of, say, a gramophone-record or a chair or beauty or justice or anything else is always going to differ slightly from the next fellow's. Agreement on the abstractions which underlie meaning, as on everything else in language, is only approximate from one speaker to the next; but we get along together anyhow, because our experience of real life and the abstractions we base on it are roughly equivalent. They can acquire greater exactitude in their equivalence only if the various speakers involved arrive at them by the same processes. This is the basic aim of scientific method, to ensure that all who are discussing a given phenomenon or set of phenomena will follow the same procedures and hence arrive at the same abstraction—but, still, each inside his own head. (Written formulas and the like do not constitute an exception to this statement. As we shall see later, whatever a scientist or any-one else may write down is only a reflection of something spoken internally, whether vocalized or only sub-vocalized.)

Similarly, absolutism or normativism of any kind are inimical to science. This fact has long since been recognized in most

[7]

fields, especially in the physical and biological sciences; at present, no-one outside of a country with a totalitarian dictatorship would think of forcing scientists to make their findings conform with any one doctrine (as did, say, Lysenko in Soviet genetics). In language, however, our belief in "correctness," establishing norms of usage which are set forth in grammar-books, taught in our schools, and perpetuated in our folk-lore, has rendered it and unfortunately still renders it difficult for members of our culture to take a scientifically based attitude towards language. Linguistic norms of course exist; however, they have no basis in the facts of language itself, but are, as we shall see, wholly derived from non-linguistic, socially determined attitudes. The distinction between "correct" and "incorrect" (or "grammatical" and "ungrammatical," "well-formed" or "ill-formed," or whatever other pair of terms we may choose to use or invent) is not only of no use, but quite harmful to the scientific study of linguistic phenomena in and for themselves.

At this point, when the lines have been clearly drawn between what is and what is not scientific, an unfortunate polarization, between "idealism" and "positivism," is often brought into the debate. (This polarization is especially common in, though by no means restricted to, the field of Romance linguistics.) By the fallacy of the excluded mean, it is assumed that if any-one is not on the side of "idealism," he must be a "positivist." This latter term is often taken to mean one who has little or no sense of spiritual truth, beauty, or the finer things of life, and whose attention is fixed entirely on "mere facts," beyond which he sees no broader or deeper significance. To counter this type of misunderstanding, we may consider a parameter of approaches to the examination of observed phenomena (adapted from G. Bachelard):

idealism—rationalism—formalism—scientific analysis—realism—
positivism—empiricism.

[8]

Scientific analysis is in the middle, combining realism (careful attention to observed reality and its inherent patterning) with enough formalism to permit of efficient and economic description of our findings. If we take formalism as an end in itself, it is easy to consider our formulas as the embodiment of abstract "reason", thus passing to rationalism; and it is only one step more to the "idealist" position that the formulas exist quite apart from reality, in an "ideal" world from which they come forth to be embodied in a corporeal form predetermined by their non-physical source. In the other direction, exclusive attention to the analysis of facts, to the neglect of the patterns of relationship among them, leads to positivism, beyond which a further neglect of analysis itself brings us to the blinkered myopia of empiricism. The facile opposition of "idealism" and "positivism" is obviously mistaken, since at the other end of the parameter from idealism is its true opposite, empiricism. Both of these approaches are equally to be condemned, idealism because it eliminates completely the basis of our studies in reality, and empiricism because it neglects that analysis and formulation of patterns inherent in observed reality which is the essence of scientific work.

One consequence of a scientific approach to human life is a reorientation—which, for many people in our culture, is quite radical—of our view of the relation between the individual on the one hand and his society and his culture on the other. The notion that society and culture are entities existing apart from and independently of the individual human beings who are their "exponents" ("the whole is greater than the sum of its parts") is very widespread, but quite unjustified by reality. It is easy to conclude, from such expressions as "society imposes sanctions upon deviant members" or "our culture inculcates certain attitudes", that a society of a culture must be something with independent characteristics and a will of its own. However, such expressions are only metaphorical and must not be taken literally. The fact is that no society, no culture, and no other collectivity ("nation," "people," "folk," etc.) exists apart from the individuals

[9]

who make it up. If any-one wishes to contradict this statement, to assert "Yes, collectivities do have independent existence," the burden of proof is on him, to demonstrate (without violating "Occam's razor," already mentioned) that we must postulate their existence to explain otherwise unexplainable facts. Show me a collectivity of any sort with a real, demonstrable existence—not just as an unobservable spirit or an impalpable miasma somehow hovering over and entering into the members of a group, but as a graspable, analyzable, formulable reality—and I will accept the fact of its existence. Until such a time, we are justified in rejecting all analyses based on the assumption that any collectivity or collective phenomenon (e.g. a linguistic system) exists in and for itself.

This denial of the existence of collectivities and collective phenomena causes us, further, to reorient our understanding of individuals and their relation to each other. As is well known, no individual human is ever exactly identical with any other, in physical, psychological, or cultural characteristics. Finger-prints are the obvious example, but our assertion is equally valid for all other features of each human being's constitution and behavior. Similarities, often (as between "identical" twins) very close, exist in great number; but similarity is not identity, unless we choose deliberately to use the term *same* to cover also the meaning of "similar," as Leonard Bloomfield did in his Postulates. It is by virtue of their close similarities that humans can interact with each other, particularly in the use of language in any given speech-community. But when we identify similarities between individuals, and contrive terms or formulas by which to refer to these similarities, we are setting up abstractions which, in their very nature, do not cover all of reality. The "collective unconscious," also, can have no real existence, since, even if we accept the hypothesis that the unconscious exists as a real part of human psychology, nothing collective exists at all. In Edward Sapir's well known remark à propos of grammatical categories and their meanings:

> It is almost as though at some period in the past the uncon-
> scious mind of the race had made a hasty inventory of experi-
> ence, committed itself to a premature classification that
> allowed of no revision, and saddled the inheritors of its lan-
> guage with a science that they no longer quite believed in
> nor had the strength to overthrow,

the scientific value of his statement is saved by the redeeming
"as though" with which he had the sense to introduce his observation. Not all philosophers of language are this intelligent
or cautious.

"Yet," some-one may object, "no individual human ever lives
wholly alone throughout his life, but forms (at some time, and in
the case of almost every-one, virtually all the time) a part of
some community. Furthermore, it is common knowledge that
people in the mass behave differently from the way they do
when they are alone. Don't we have to assume some special
factor to account for these differences in behavior?" The answer
is: definitely not. Of course ordinary people live all their lives
in the company of others, and are profoundly influenced thereby;
man is certainly a social animal, even if he is not *the* social animal
par excellence. When people are in groups, each person's behavior is surely influenced by the presence of others; yet the
variations in behavior are due to changes in individual attitudes
and inhibitions, not to the generation of some extra-individual
collective spiritual or psychological force. The *locus existendi* of
all human behavior and its physical or psychological sources is
only inside each separate body. (This is true even of the most
intimate form of social interaction, sexual intercourse. When
Jesus said "husband and wife are one flesh," he was establishing
an ideal for people to behave *as if* it were true, not stating a
physiological fact.) Donne's metaphysical observation "No man
is an island" was, in fact, the exact opposite of the truth. Every
man is an island—with, indeed, many, many bridges to other
men's islands, as it were—and remains an island from birth to
death.

[11]

When an individual lives, as we all normally do, in society with others, he is subject to all kinds of pressures, enforced by sanctions or coercion, to behave in approved ways and to refrain from behaving in disapproved ones. Many anthropologists and sociologists speak of such pressures as being brought by "the society" or "the culture." Yet, here again, these pressures, as embodied in approving or disapproving attitudes and manifested in specific actions (or the absence thereof), exist only in the individual behavior of individual people. If I do something of which my society (i.e. the people around me) approves highly, such as rescuing a person from danger, it will show its approval exclusively through individual actions ranging from smiles (from specific, identifiable people) to a medal or a cash award (also bestowed by particular individuals). If, on the other hand, I do something bad, I may be punished, by any type of sanction ranging from mere frowns to execution, but again exerted only by specific persons, even when they do so in the name of abstract institutions such as "the state" or "the law." Any claim to speak or to mete out approval or disapproval in the name of a collectivity (which, as we have seen, can have no existence in real fact) is either naïve or else fraudulent, as when, in Stalinist times, the Russian cultural dictator Zhdanov condemned Shostakovich's *Lady Macbeth of Mzensk* "in the name of the entire Soviet people." Much of the intra- and international upheaval of our times has been caused by fanatics and politicians who reify fictional collectivities and claim falsely to be entitled to voice their imaginary "aspirations" ("the —— people's right to independent sovereignty" and the like).

The "individualism" set forth here, i.e. the recognition that in all human groups only individuals exist, is of course not to be confused with a low-level pseudo-philosophical out-look also called "individualism," the view that individuals have obligations only towards themselves and are therefore entitled to disregard all principles of morality and behave in a wholly selfish way towards other people. Of course each individual, in his life together with others, has relations with them, feelings towards them, and moral obligations with regard to them. But these relations, feelings, and obligations, real though they are, exist only in the individual himself, and in the other individuals with whom he is in direct or indirect contact. This is true all the way from personal relations to the duty of each of us towards our "nation," i.e. towards all our fellow citizens, and towards the human race in general. If the tender-minded reader is offended by these statements, we may point out that they do not render our affections, obligations, and duties, in short all the emotional and moral side of our existence, any less real. They simply place them on a different, and to one observer's way of thinking, more objective basis.

In relation to his culture and his language, therefore, each individual has his own set of patterns, which, as already mentioned, are extremely similar to and overlap almost (though never absolutely) entirely with those of the other individuals in the same community. For the individual's total set of linguistic patterns, the term *idiolect* has been devised. No such parallel term has yet achieved general acceptance to refer to the totality of an individual's set of cultural patterns; on earlier occasions, I have referred to them as an *idiocult;* the term *idioverse,* also somewhat awkward, has recently been proposed. In any case, the idiocult is the only ultimate analytical reality in culture, as is the idiolect in language. Even the idiocult and the idiolect are of course abstractions, in that each of them is the totality of an individual's patterns of activity. We can get at an idiocult or an idiolect—as we can get at the totality of an individual's activity in any other respect—only by observation of his activities. In practice, given the inevitable limitations on the time and energy of each one of us, and on the number of persons available to work in any field of research, we have to depend on sampling-techniques, and assume that our sample is large enough and well enough distributed to be representative of what we are studying. For the further abstractions of "culture" or of "dialect" and "language," we have to rely even more on sampling-techniques,

[13]

in that it would be quite impossible to observe in minute detail the doings of every member of every human community all the time. So we assume that a given number of individuals will be representative of the group as a whole, and study their activities enough to assure ourselves that we have attained at least a reasonably valid statistical norm. (Note well, however, that no norm attained in this way ever has a basis in anything more than statistical frequency.)

Given these limitations on both the nature of our object of study (humans and their activities) and the kind of observations we can make, what are the types of techniques we can use? Direct examination first of all, of course, and recording of our findings—in the case of language, listening to what people say and "taking it down" by whatever means we have available (usually with pencil and paper, or else with mechanical recording-devices), or, with documents of past speech, reading and interpreting whatever has been left to us in one kind of notation or another. As is well known, there are limitations on the usefulness of direct examination by only the observer's five senses, since these are notoriously insufficient to penetrate to all the characteristics of the objects of our study. Any mechanical device, therefore, which enables us to extend and either confirm or correct the findings of our senses, is welcome—in linguistics, especially in the field of phonetics (kymograph, sound-spectrograph, speech-stretcher, etc.). Further analysis, re-ordering, and formulation of our findings is an essential part of our work. It must not be thought, however, that "discovery-procedures" (as they have on occasion, more or less sneeringly, been called) are foreign to scientific work. In other words, one cannot come to anthropology, linguistics, or any other science armed only with a naïve native user's knowledge of the culture, language, or other object of study, and without getting rid of the folk-lore which, in our and probably in every other culture, attaches to and largely obscures the actual facts to be observed.

Controlled experiment is, in many branches of science, possible because their object of study is relatively limited, with a relatively small range and few parameters of variation, and the span of time involved in experimentation is relatively short. In examining human activities, however, the object of our study is vast, with extensive differences and a great number of variables. In some sub-divisions of anthropology and linguistics, the time-span is short, but in others it is extremely long, covering many decades or (in the case of historical linguistics and philology) centuries and millennia. Even in those instances where the time-span is short enough to permit one observer to carry out his investigations during his life-time, there are often all kinds of social pressures and taboos militating against his setting up a controlled experiment which would involve imposing outwardly dictated variations on the lives of the persons whose activities he might wish to observe and record. Under these circumstances, the social scientist is in a position which resembles that of the geologist or the astronomer rather than the physicist or the chemist. He must take as much material as he can get, through the gathering of uncontrolled samples (such as chance and the willingness of his fellow-humans may allow him to observe), and such controlled experimentation as the time at his disposal and the nature of his subject may permit; and he must then fill in what is not available to direct observation by establishing hypotheses to be tested as occasion permits.

The place of scientific hypotheses, subject to verification, can never be taken, however, by any kind of speculation, of a rationalistic or aprioristic kind, unanchored to the observation of reality. "It stands to reason that . . ." is no argument to be used in any kind of scientific work, since "reason" or "logic" does not exist in the abstract (as we have already seen), and ideas of what is or what is not rational or logical will inevitably differ from one culture to another, and from the users of one linguistic structure to those of another. One of the basic aims of a scientific approach is to discover patterns of reality which are independent of the culture and the linguistic structure of any observer. Hence all

[15]

the emphasis which, as we have seen, is placed upon objectivity, impersonality, and the possibility of a scientific discovery being made as many times as desired by observers independently of each other and of their allegiance to any given nation, culture, or language. Mathematics, likewise, although it can be useful to anthropology or linguistics in an ancillary way, can never be at the center of any basic study of human activities. This is because mathematics is only a generalized type of linguistic behavior, and is in the last analysis subject to the same limitations as those we have already noted for a "rational" approach.

One final non-linguistic point remains to be made, concerning the relation of synchronic to diachronic study. This topic has occasioned much spilling of ink: many articles and even books have been written, in the field of linguistics alone, over the relation of the synchronic and the diachronic view-points. Some (like de Saussure) have maintained that the two were absolutely irreconcilable, others (like von Wartburg) have tried to reconcile them. The entire polemic ceases to be meaningful as soon as we realize that a purely synchronic view-point rests on a fiction, the pretense that it is possible to observe a phenomenon and to describe it without time passing at all during the act of observation and description. In actual fact, time is always passing, even while we are observing something, and—be it in ever so slight a way—the object of our study is always changing. Nevertheless, this fiction is useful (as witness the reliance we all place on such results of synchronic description as maps, charts, and time-tables), and it is well to retain it, provided we do not allow it to influence our techniques of observation or our methods of analysis. (If we do, we run the risk of presenting human activity in a lifeless form, as if it were comparable to the cadavers which medical students observe in a dissecting-room.) Similarly, it will be useful to introduce—as in our next few chapters—an achronic point of view, ascribing general, timeless validity to what has been repeatedly observed as happening innumerable times to countless millions of humans.

[16]

2

THE "LIFE-CYCLE" OF THE IDIOLECT

It is customary to say that languages, since they are not organisms of any kind, do not have life-cycles; and this is certainly
true. Nor can we speak, except metaphorically, of languages
"being born" or "dying," or of "mother-languages" and "daughter-
languages." Yet each idiolect is related to the events that characterize its user's life-span, and hence we can say that the idiolect
has a kind of life-cycle. We can, therefore, set up an over-all
description for the path of inception, development, and extinction
the normal idiolect follows during the life of its user.

The baby, at birth, does not speak; it is *infans*, "not speaking".
Of course its brain is not a *tabula rasa* in the absolute. There are
certain in-born, genetically conditioned capacities, and also limitations, with which the new-born infant is endowed. One of these
capacities is that of symbolization, the ability to use one phenomenon (object, action, relationship) to stand for another, and
thus to correlate many things in quite extensive ways with simple
means. Human communication depends on this ability, not only
in oral-auditory language, but in all the other ways by which we
convey meanings through symbols (e.g. flowers, punctuality, dis-
tance between members of a group, or even the position of a
postage-stamp on a letter). Another capacity is that of forming
patterns by analogy, and still another is that of forming habits.
The baby is also endowed by his heredity with certain organs in
his respiratory system, which serve him later in the utterance of

sounds, and in his auditory system, which are used in interpreting the sounds he hears.

Symbolization, the ability to form patterns and habits, and the organs of speech and hearing: these aspects of the infant's heredity exhaust the list of the genetically determined features which he will use in language. All the evidence available to date indicates that these characteristics are the same in all normal humans, without difference according to racial groups or cultural level. There is also no evidence to support the allegation that capacity to produce one type of sound or another is conditioned by racial inheritance or any other factor, e.g. blood-type. The instance usually cited in disproof of such allegations is the common observation that children of any race, blood-type, etc., brought up in a speech-community different from that of their physical parents will show all the linguistic characteristics of the group they are brought up in (e.g. people of Japanese origin in the United States speak completely normal American English; children of white missionaries in Africa use the local African languages exactly as do the natives; and so on).

Nor can it be said that the infant has any kind of linguistic structure born in him, except in the most general sense of having the ability to establish correlations between a symbol and what it stands for, i.e. its meaning. That there is any inherent "deep structure" inborn in a child's linguistic equipment, is an unfounded and undemonstrable assertion, based on a theory invented *ad hoc* to explain certain otherwise indefensible, aprioristic assumptions of a neo-rationalistic approach to linguistics (cf. Chapter 5). The capacity to develop and use the faculty of language is inborn in every normal human, but not the particular structural or semantic characteristics his idiolect or other system of communication will assume. These will be determined by those of the speech-community in which fate or chance has placed him, i.e. of the people with whom he will grow up and live in daily contact. Dante's formulation, in the *Divina Commedia* (*Paradiso* 26. 130–132), is still valid:

[18]

Opera naturale è ch'uom favella;
ma così o così, natura lascia
poi fare a voi secondo che v'abbella.

"It is a result of the way that he is born that man speaks; but whether this way or that, Nature then leaves it up to you, as best suits your fancy."

Immediately after birth, the baby cries; and he soon begins to babble. At first, he makes all kind of noises, more or less at random; later, however, certain types disappear, so that it has been observed that an infant's repertory of sounds at, say, six months is often considerably smaller than it was at one or two months. It has been suggested that this reduction is due to the baby's beginning to accommodate the sounds he makes to those he hears from people around him, as they speak in his presence. In any case, this babbling constitutes an essential preparation for the child's linguistic development, since it provides it with its initial practice in managing and coördinating its organs of speech. Parents and others around the child actively further this process, speaking to it and acting as informants, often in a conventionalized, reduced form of baby-talk. Random babbling gradually shades off into patterned sound correlated with some identifiable feature of the context, i.e. into meaningful speech, usually beginning around the sixth or eighth month, but in some cases not until the twelfth month or even later. There is some evidence to show that intonational features are the first to make their appearance, followed later by phonemic contrasts involving two or more phonemes (e.g. *baba, dada*).

The child's contact with and use of language is thus conditioned, from the earliest stages, by cultural transmission, in that he always imitates the actions of those around him. (No-one has ever demonstrated the existence of any in-born mechanism whereby every child produces specific sequences of sounds with specific meanings at the same stage of development.) Whether the ability to imitate is an in-born trait of humans, as is the ability

[19]

to form patterns and habits, is still a subject of debate: some psychologists consider it innate, others regard it as learned. In any case, it is well known that there is an optimum stage for children to learn their first language through direct imitation of other humans. If this stage is passed without language-habits being acquired, the child's ability to do so can be gravely impaired.

At the very first stage of child language, each utterance constitutes a separate morpheme (is *monomorphemic*), without any necessary similarity to the rest of the child's (at this stage) quite limited stock of morphemes. The child has a set of phonemes, two or more, out of which the stock of morphemes is built; we are thus entitled to say that duality between the phonological and the morphological levels begins as soon as the child starts to talk intelligibly at all. A syntactic level, and with it productivity, does not start until a second stage is reached, at which the child forms new utterances out of existing ones, by recombining their parts on the basis of analogy (e.g. on the basis of *daddy come, mommy come,* and *daddy all gone,* producing *mommy all gone* without ever having heard any-one else say this last). The ability to analogize is apparently in-born; but the actual patterns by which a child forms new utterances are not. They are learned through observation and imitation of others. All through the monomorphemic stage and the earlier steps of the polymorphemic stages (which lasts all the rest of the individual's life, except in cases of aphasia due to brain-damage or -deterioration), the child's imitation of his models is often quite aberrant, and it is only through a process of trial-and-error that he gradually arrives at a closer approximation (though, as we have said, never complete identity).

Due to the extensive operation of analogy, immediately after the child has passed out of the monomorphemic into the polymorphemic stage, his use of language becomes highly productive, in that he becomes able to produce utterances which neither he nor his hearers have ever heard before, and to understand such

utterances when he hears them from others. At first, his stock of
morphemes and of syntactic structures is relatively slight, and
does not correspond to those of fully developed adult usage. In
a few years, however, the child's morphology and syntax come
rapidly closer to those of the normal speech of the community,
so that by the age of five or six he is able to produce extensive
and complex sentences, with all but a few analogical "errors"
(e.g. *foots* for *feet*) ironed out. The process involved is essentially
that of the combination of a relatively few, fairly simple structural types into more extensive utterances, through the inclusion
of some types within others by processes of coördination and sub-
ordination. During the process of learning these structural types,
the child always makes analogical extensions, many of them quite
intelligent (*mans* for *men, breaked* for *broke,* etc.), and has to
learn by experience—i.e. by being corrected by other people—how
far he can go in such analogical new-formation. It is analogy that
lies at the base of productivity in our use of language. The work-
ings of analogy are sufficient to explain the development of each
person's idiolect, and we do not need to assume the "flowering"
of any already existent, innate linguistic system. The child learns
through imitation and analogical construction, not by rules. If,
in some varieties of linguistics, the analyst establishes sets of
rules which he calls the "grammar" of a child's or an adult's
language, such a grammar is a purely abstract construct, and
there is no guarantee that the sequence of such rules corresponds
in the slightest to the process by which the child learns his native
language or to that by which a speaker produces his utterances.

Nor is there any "creativity" involved in the child's learning
to use a phonological, morpho-syntactic, and semantic system. As
for the system itself, he is simply building up inside himself a
set of patterned habits, by imitation of, first his parents and the
immediate members of his family, and then his play-mates and
others with whom he comes in contact. He learns to produce
novel utterances, but novelty is not the same as creativity.
Creativity would imply the invention and production of linguistic

features or elements never heard before, such as absolutely fresh sentence-types or absolutely unfamiliar morphemes and meanings for them. Tens or hundreds of thousands of years ago, there must have been extensive creation of this type, but that stage of human linguistic history has long since been passed. In each individual's linguistic development, if he does create absolutely new morphemes, structures, or meanings, such creativity is quickly repressed. The child learns quite early that anything he may invent *ex novo* stands little enough chance of being accepted by his immediate family and virtually none in the rest of the speech-community. In fact, as has often been remarked, a good part of a child's *iter* in acquiring his native language consists of discovering what features his interlocutors consider non-essential to comprehension and in learning to turn, first metaphorically and then almost literally, a deaf ear to them.

Together with the patterns of sounds, forms, and combinations thereof, the child learns the meanings associated with them in his native language. In other words, he learns to set up correlations between the phenomena of linguistic structure and those of the non-linguistic world. Two points need to be made here: (1) that the child learns these meanings, as he learns the rest of his language, only gradually; and (2) that he learns them, not only for individual lexical items, but for the morphological and syntactical aspects of linguistic structure and (insofar as they are present) for such features of phonology as intonation-patterns. Especially in the initial stages, the child learns new meanings only by direct experience: he finds out with regard to which situations one does and does not use a word, construction, etc. Since this earliest stage takes place wholly outside of awareness, and is normally not remembered when the child becomes an adult, it is easy for the individual, later on, to regard the most essential meanings (e.g. those of intonations or of basic sentence-types) as something predetermined and virtually God-given in his language. Later, when he has acquired an extensive enough vocabulary, he can learn the meanings of new items (especially

[22]

lexical) by definition rather than direct experience. With the aspects of language that do not have meanings in and for themselves—i.e. sound-types and their patternings—their learning and reproduction normally goes on outside of awareness at all times, even when the adolescent or young adult acquires a new accent (see below). Hence it becomes virtually impossible to convince the naïve monolingual native speaker of a language that there is either any necessity or any usefulness in analyzing its phonology.

When he has built up a fully-grown idiolect as part of his patterns of reacting to his environment, the individual uses it for two purposes. The most obvious purpose is that of communicating with those with whom he comes in contact, acting as both receiver and sender of messages. In any given speech-community, no two individuals' idiolects are absolutely identical, any more than are their finger-prints. But they are closely similar, enough so as to permit of extensive (though never, in the nature of human affairs, perfect) mutual understanding and interaction. To many, this has seemed to be not only the prime, but the sole function of language. Certainly, without social organization, and especially without others in the immediate family whom the child can imitate, modelling his idiolect on what he hears from them, no-one could build up a set of linguistic patterns, in either form or meaning. Yet the idiolect has another function, at least equally important: that of serving as a part, and a most important part, of the mechanism whereby a person's memory functions. By means of language, telling ourselves things and memorizing complete or partial utterances (of our own or other people's), we are able to bridge much greater gaps in time or space than non-speaking animals. (This is especially true in literate societies, where we can note down what we want to remember, but it is also true in non-literate communities—in these latter, in fact, people's memories for both shorter and longer utterances is much better developed than in the former.) Furthermore, every person is speaking to himself all the time (with subvocalization if not with overt speech), so that a great part of what we call

[23]

"thought" would be impossible without an individual's use of his idiolect to talk things over with himself.

So far, we have been describing a process which goes on for every normal human child, in every speech-community. (The fact that substitute-processes take place for non-normal children, e.g. deaf-mutes or spastics, does not render our description invalid for the great mass of humanity.) It is wholly auditory and oral in its nature, depending in no way upon the use of visual symbolism or representation, nor upon paralinguistic features (gestures, etc.), although it is normally associated with behavior involving these latter. If paralinguistic features were essential to human communication by means of speech, it would not be possible for the users of every language, even the most "primitive," to talk to each other around corners or on the telephone. Perhaps half the members of the human race, even today, continue for the rest of their lives to speak and listen to each other, with no use of writing at all; and this was the case, up to a few hundred years ago, for at least nine-tenths of the people born into so-called "advanced" cultures. In our modern world, however, in the countries where education is (at least nominally) universal, the child is sent to school at the age of five or six, and picks up at least a nodding acquaintance, usually considerably more, with the writing-system that is habitually used in connection with his language. The knowledge which he thus acquires exerts a strong and lasting influence, not so much on his use of the language itself in every-day speech, but on his notions and attitudes concerning both his own language and language in general.

For the child in early school-age, attention is concentrated, not upon his speaking-activity (which both he and his teachers, and every-one with whom he discusses such matters, take for granted), but on the acquisition of writing-habits, and the restrictions associated with their use. The variety of the language to be used in writing is normally, in virtually every speech-community, different in at least some respects from every-day usage, and the child is subjected to extensive and continued discussion of these respects. He learns to regard the "written language" as superior to the "spoken form" and prior to it in both importance and origin. He learns to regard his own and others' use of language in terms of school-book rules, and to consider any variation therefrom as the result of "corruption," of deliberate disobedience or else of lazy disregard of what he "ought" to do in both speaking and writing. At some point in his education—early in most countries, later in others—the child is introduced to works of literature through reading and class discussion. The study of literature is in itself excellent, and highly to be commended; unfortunately, it is often used as a pretext for teaching the pupils further inaccurate notions, such as that there is a positive correlation between the use of a given linguistic feature in literature and its intrinsic worth.

Whether he goes to school or not, however, the child, even as early as six or seven years of age, becomes aware that those around him expect him to speak in certain particular ways and not in others. In every speech-community that has been investigated, some usages are regarded as more effective than others and hence preferable, and, since every language is always changing, some usages are on their way out and others coming in. Even if he has not been to school and hence has not been taught to venerate the prescriptions of some grammar-book or dictionary, the speaker of a language unreflectingly acquires the idea that, outside of himself, there exist standards by which his linguistic behavior can be measured. For the naïve untutored speaker, it is easy to ascribe a real existence to these standards, and for the pupil in school, they do seem to have a basis in the prescriptive attitudes he is almost inevitably taught towards his language. In fact, however, they are, even for the most illiterate "savage," existent only as an abstraction which he has set up more or less unreflectingly on the basis of his observations of others in his community. Using the term *super-ego*, not in the narrow Freudian sense of one's father-image, but in the more general meaning of "what one thinks one's fellow humans expect one to be and do", we may call this abstraction the *linguistic super-ego*. Although it has no real existence outside of each speaker's notions about his own language, it nevertheless exerts considerable influence on his attitudes and behavior, and on his reactions towards other people's use of his language. The type of linguistic super-ego fostered in the child can differ markedly from one community to another, ranging from extreme permissivity and nearly total indifference (as in most speakers of Australian English) to the opposite extreme of rigorous insistence on conformity (as in many educated Frenchmen).

The child's ability to acquire new patterns of linguistic behavior seems to be at its greatest between the ages of, say, one and eight. Between these ages, he is receptive and imitative. Many children (more than is often thought) are bilingual from the out-set, even though they usually end up having more extensive and effective command of one of their languages than the other. Even in the case of those who start to acquire a second language only after having mastered the "blood and bone" of their first by, say, five or six years of age, their success in imitating the sounds and forms of the second one is much greater if they begin before they are eight or so. There is some evidence that this is due to a greater innate capacity of the brain: the individual's linguistic adaptability is very great at the out-set but diminishes from the ninth year or so onwards. (This is, of course, a major argument for the study of foreign languages from the earliest stages of elementary school, so as to get the learner started while he is still at his most adaptable.) From eight or so onward, however, the individual—especially if he is monolingual and comes in contact only with members of his own speech-community—rapidly becomes "sot in his ways" as far as his language-habits are concerned. The "hardening-process" goes on apace, so that by the time they are, say, twelve, most people are already linguistic adults.

From this time on, also, the development of new linguistic habits slows down markedly, although it never stops entirely.

The speaker's ability to learn whole new systems becomes very much less, although this phenomenon varies markedly from one individual to another. Some become almost entirely sunk in the ruts of their native linguistic patterns. For such persons, it becomes extremely hard to learn a new language, and they even rebel actively against the suggestion that other languages can be as reasonable or as natural as their own. At the other extreme are those who retain a special facility, as contrasted with others, in picking up new language-habits, even to an advanced age. It may be surmised that these differences in language-learning-ability are connected with attitudes towards the semantic content and the structure of one's native tongue, and with inhibitions against behaving in linguistically unfamiliar ways. The first-mentioned type seem to be concerned almost exclusively with the meaning of what they have to say, so much so that they almost resent attention to the linguistic form in which they consider it as being "cast," as a needless and meaningless distraction. The second type are often interested in the use of linguistic structure for its own sake, at least in practice if not always in analytical terms, and are exceptionally uninhibited in being willing to make strange sounds and strange combinations of forms, with strange meanings, even if those around them are not always so willing.

The adaptability-factor remains relatively great, for most individuals, with respect to dialectal variations, up to the age of twenty or twenty-two. There are a great many instances in which persons move from one region of a country to another and take on features of the dialect-area into which they have moved, doing so with relative ease. Children moving at an early age simply lose their first dialect (especially its phonological features) and acquire the new one, as my children did when moving from New England to up-state New York at the ages of five and three respectively. The ability to adapt one's speech in this way remains present, however, at least up to college-age, so that many students, on leaving (say) New York state to go to college in Ohio, take on features of Ohio speech. The more adaptable may retain

[27]

both dialects, and be able to shift from one to the other depending on the environment they are in; others may simply retain such features of the new one as they have taken on, so that their idiolects become quite mixed. This process is one of the major sources of dialect-mixture, especially in countries where (as in the United States) population-mobility is great. Linguistically sophisticated persons may remain dialectally adaptable long after their early twenties, so that here, also, it is impossible to fix a single developmental point at which adaptability ceases.

In the mean-while, the individual has gone on acquiring new linguistic features all the time, especially lexical items. As is well known, even in a "primitive" culture no one individual comes to be totally proficient in all the activities that are carried on by every-one in the community, so that there are always special branches of knowledge and of the vocabulary which any given individual can keep coming into fresh contact with. If the community is differentiated dialectally to any extent, he may also meet structural features different from his own, e.g. "funny" verb-forms like *clim, clam,* or *clum* for "climbed", or the use of *need* or *dare* as modal auxiliaries (*Need you do that?—Yes, I need.*) Whether he accepts these or not depends very largely on non-linguistic factors, especially his attitude towards those from whom he hears the novelties. If he dislikes the people who have introduced him to such new features, considering them socially inferior in any way ("trash," "country bumpkins," or the like) or self-appointedly superior ("snobs," "la-di-da," etc.), he may reject the innovations, often retaining a passive knowledge of them but refusing to use them himself. Typical of this attitude is the remark of an old gentleman in one of Scott's novels: "What's wrong with the world nowadays, sir, is all these demmed new words. Too many demmed new words!". (As time passes, though, he may come to use them, outside of awareness, and even denying overtly that he uses them at all.) At the other extreme of this scale of willingness to accept innovations, we have enthusiastic adoption—more common, in our society, among the young than among the old, and shading off into use of slang. By *slang* we normally mean forms or meanings which come into use very quickly, are extremely popular and have a very high frequency of occurrence for a relatively short time (from a few months to a year or two) and then—usually, but not always—drop out of use as fast as they came in. Most individuals' attitudes fall somewhere between these two extremes.

In our modern world, with its rapid (and increasing) rate of technological innovation, even the hill-billy's or the slum-dweller's exposure to new vocabulary continues strong all through his life. If it were possible to take a complete inventory of any individual's vocabulary at, say, five-year intervals, we might, through a number of such studies, calculate the average speaker's receptivity and percentage of increase over the decades. All we can say at the present is that no idiolect can possibly remain absolutely static, particularly under modern conditions. We can at least guess that the individual's rate of vocabulary-acquisition would normally diminish with the years; but this may be off-set nowadays by the increasing amount of new terminology to which even the "senior citizens" are exposed whether they like it or not.

By the time he is in his twenties, therefore, the individual has developed the ability to use an extensive repertory of sounds, forms, syntactical combinations, and lexical items. It has become customary to call this ability his "competence"—a term with which there need be no quarrel, as long as it is not reified and ascribed some kind of existence in the abstract. As we shall see in Chapter 4, this competence is not perfect or in complete equilibrium at any point in the history of any individual's idiolect: it is constantly changing in one respect or another, even though such changes may often be in extremely minor matters. Consequently, it is not at all justified to think of the individual's competence as growing until it reaches a point of perfection, standing still for a time, and then declining. The individual's competence exists in him and with respect to his own idiolect; it is not part of some over-all system existing outside of himself, and hence

[29]

it is not subject to any kind of "rules" which an analyst may set up to describe a synchronically fictional "dialect" or "language." Against my point of view, it may be argued that the user of a standard language (especially one like French which has been extensively codified and "regulated") is only following in his own usage the rules of a system which has an objective existence in prescriptive grammars and in "good" literature. Here, too, however, we may reply that the prescriptive grammars and dictionaries codify only a part (never the whole) of what has been written, only in one particular literary variety, and that the written corpus which they purport to codify is in fact the reflection of its authors' idiolects. These, in their turn, are simply normal idiolects like every-one else's, no matter how much their users may think they are conforming to some standard imposed from outside (i.e. no matter how over-grown and tyrannical their linguistic super-egos may be).

What happens to an idiolect as its user grows old is, to a large extent, conditioned by his life-history, and by the particular accidents that may befall his brain or his organs of hearing and speech. At one extreme, we have persons who retain their ability to hear others' speech and to respond, and remain intellectually active, up to an extremely advanced age. At the other are those who, due to senility or brain-injury or haemorrhage, lose the faculty of speech and/or understanding, either completely or in part. In between these two extremes lie the great majority of speakers, who retain reasonable command of their linguistic faculties up to the end or nearly so. Various factors may interfere with successful performance, quite aside from what may happen to the individual's competence itself: for instance, a person may lose so many teeth that clarity of enunciation is impaired; deafness (total or partial) may impair both hearing and feed-back on one's own performance; or disease (such as cancer of the tongue) may impair use of the speech-organs. In general, the amount of energy used in hearing and speaking is so small that even a person who has been badly injured in an accident, or whose energies have almost totally disappeared so far as gross corporeal motions are concerned, can still retain the ability to speak and hear, provided there has been no actual brain-damage. It is often remarked that, if some-one is too weak even to speak, he must be very far gone indeed.

Even when real decline has set in, it cannot be said that the idiolect follows an exclusively downward curve, with the individual simply losing more and more of his competence until it disappears altogether at his death. In both non-linguistic and linguistic respects, one's memory may, at any time, bring back experiences or behavior-patterns that have remained forgotten for years or even decades. This is said to happen particularly as individuals feel that the end is near, and they start to recall their early childhood, remembering persons, places, and early learning-experiences that they had thought totally forgotten. (This is another reason why one really cannot count the number of lexical items or other features in any given idiolect, because there is no telling when any given word, etc., may suddenly recur to memory and come into use again.)

The extinction of any given individual's idiolect comes only when he permanently loses the faculty of responding to speech and of speaking—normally at death, occasionally before. What survives afterwards is simply a record of part of the idiolect, whether it be in the form of more or less extensive written documents (until recently, the only means for preserving an at least partial indication of what some-one has said), or in that of more direct preservation, e.g. by gramophone-record, tape- or wire-recording, or talking film. Since, as is well known, any speaker is able to produce a number of different utterances limited only by his energy and the time available to him in his life-span, no such record can ever be more than partial, even in the case of such voluminous writers as Balzac or Henry James. A study of the totality of such a writer's language would give us a picture that, no matter how detailed it were made, could only be asymptotic to the total range of possibilities. Often we have the impression that

[31]

the history of a language is continuous, and therefore constitutes a study which can be exhaustive. Such an impression, however, is due only to the fact that the available corpus, for modern literary languages like French or English, is so extensive. Yet, however extensive it may be, it is never more than a partial representation of its authors' idiolects, and they in their turn have constituted only a small fraction of the totality of the speech-behavior of their communities, i.e. of the idiolects of all the speakers that have lived and died in them.

3

LANGUAGE IN SOCIETY

As we saw in the first chapter, "society" does not exist apart from the individuals that make it up, and consequently no "social" manifestation is anything but individual in nature. When we speak of language as being both an individual and a social phenomenon, all that we mean by this is that each person uses language both for communication with other persons and as part of his own memory. Yet this does not constitute a denial that people live together in society, or that language is the chief bond that holds them together and enables them to coöperate. As long as we realize the abstract nature of any unity ("dialect", "language", "society") beyond the level of the individual, and keep this fact in mind all the time, we are perfectly justified in discussing these abstractions and their relations to each other.

There are of course several possible levels of abstraction, in each of which we take into consideration only the features common to more than one observed phenomenon. Of the several meanings current for the term *dialect*, the one most useful in linguistics is "abstraction based on features common to two or more idiolects". (The meanings "disfavored variety of speech", "corruption of good usage", and "foreign accent" are only confusing and harmful to scientific objectivity.) Even the features present in only two persons' speech can be abstracted and referred to as a dialect, e.g. that of a husband and wife, or any other two persons whom it may be convenient to lump together in this way. Any small group of people (e.g. a family) that associate together constantly will develop features peculiar to themselves which make it useful to speak of their dialect. Almost every family has its own dialectal characteristics, usually deriving from some common experience, such as one of its members' childish attempts at imitating adult speech: in my family, for instance, *sillo* for "cereal", *ackit* "attic", *moogis* "music", *sorter* "to sort (out)", and similar forms are still current twenty or more years after they first arose. Any other experience of one or more members of a group may leave similar traces, such as our adoption of a Russian dining-car-steward's literal translation of /súp s grivic^{j}éj/ as "soup with a hen", and our further, intentionally humorous loan-translation, on the same model, of Italian *crema di funghi* "cream of mush-rooms" as *soup with a fungus.*

The small group's dialect is popularly regarded as only the extreme reduction of the more general instance of a regional variety which has common features—e.g. the speech of a given village, city, district, or province (*el dialecto de Cabranes* or "the dialect of Cabranes", "Asturian dialect"). It is more accurate, however, to see in the dialect of a larger group a still further abstraction, based on the comparison of more and more idiolects. Instead of calling the speech of ever smaller groups "sub-dialects", "sub-sub-dialects" etc., therefore, we would do better to speak of abstractions based on the speech of larger groups as "super-dialects". Other groupings than those of two-dimensional geographical extension can constitute the bases of dialectal diversity. The best-known of these are social classes or castes ("U" vs. "non-U" in Britain, "Brahmin" vs. "non-Brahmin" in India). Especially worthy of attention are the dialects of particular professional groups, whether they are active within the frame-work of a given society (e.g. artisans) or outside it (thieves or confidence-men). In most studies on dialects, particularly of these latter types, attention is often concentrated on those features which dif-

[34]

ferentiate them from what seems to be the "normal" usage of the rest of the community. Such attention to the merely strange or picturesque, however, obscures the fact that all dialects have their own coherence and consistency, which can be observed only when all aspects of their structure are described.

Beyond the level of the family, regional, or social dialect, there is that of the "language". So many misconceptions have entered into current distinctions between idiolect, dialect, and language, that it will be best to start from the most elementary aspects of the relation between the three. From the point of view of linguistic structure, there is no difference at all involved. The idiolect of the most lowly street-sweeper of Bombay has just as much structural consistency—and hence as much right to be described by the techniques of linguistic analysis—as the dialect of the whole city, or the language of the most holy Vedic hymn. If we set up invidious distinctions between various types of speech (and virtually all people do so), it can be only on the basis of some kind of non-linguistic criterion, such as the existence of a writing-system or of a prestigious literature associated with the linguistic system in question, or its use by a socially favored group. Again, on this level as on that of the dialect, if we recognize that a "language" is an abstraction, established by means of non-linguistic criteria, we are justified in discussing it as such. In general, we recognize a language on the basis of its function as the common speech of a political group (especially, though not always, a nation), or as the vehicle of some type of literature.

There is a constant interaction taking place between each individual and the other members of his group (society, nation) with regard to linguistic behavior. Some of the factors involved are linguistic, others non-linguistic. Individuals are constantly meeting sounds, forms, constructions, lexical items that they have never or only rarely come across before. If I hear (or, in a literate society, read) something unfamiliar, there are three possibilities: I may remain indifferent to it, reject it, or adopt it if it proves

[35]

useful to me. The last-mentioned would seem to be the normal reaction of the untutored, naïve native speaker of an un-school-mastered language. (Hence the profusion of loan-words connected with modern technology, spreading from English and other European languages, which disturbs purists but which is a perfectly natural and normal phenomenon, in no way to be condemned a priori or out of hand.)

Since language and its use are virtually never free from non-linguistic influences, however, we find the latter affecting speakers' attitudes and behavior towards novelties. Pure personal likes or dislikes play a much larger rôle than is normally realized. We all—even the most "objectively" inclined linguistic analyst—have our preferences, positive or negative. Among my own *bêtes noires* are, for example, the use of *presently* meaning "at present" and *hike* for "raise, rise"; and I seem to be a minority of one in the English-speaking world in refusing to use *car* for any type of vehicle except one that runs on rails. The difference between a linguist and a naïve native speaker in matters of this kind is that the former recognizes his personal likes and dislikes for what they are; he does not fool himself into thinking that they have any validity beyond his own usage, and so does not impose them on other speakers. Beyond the level of preferences for particular items, the personality-set of an individual contributes to his attitudes towards innovations. Some persons are much more inclined than others to accept them—and, of course, often change their out-looks as time goes on, usually passing from a more liberal, free-and-easy stance to one less so.

Other people's opinions are often influential in determining an individual's attitudes, in linguistic as in other matters. In a complex modern society, in fact, it would be hard to find any-one so stubborn or single-minded as to be totally insensitive to social pressures. The simplest form of influence is that of prestige, positive or negative. Who among us has not, at one time or another, started to use a word, a construction, or a pronunciation because we heard it from some-one we liked or admired? Who has not avoided some linguistic phenomenon (e.g. *hain't* "has not", or some "dirty word") because it seemed characteristic of a person or a social group that we disliked, looked down upon, or wanted to dissociate ourselves from? If these likes or dislikes are based on wide-spread attitudes of one national group towards others, they become manifestations of xenophobia or xenophilia, as the case may be. Of the latter type are the recurrent Anglomanias that beset the French-speaking world every century or so; of the former, the violent but, on the whole, futile puristic reactions in "defense of the language" such as a certain recent campaign against "le franglais".

Often, but not always, allied to factors of social prestige are considerations of artistic use. It is a wide-spread belief that languages vary in merit, according to the degree to which they are used as vehicles for literary expression. There is no *a priori* reason why this should be so, since no such thing as an abstract criterion of beauty or aesthetic merit exists by which any linguistic phenomenon can be judged. Here again, it is either individual likes and dislikes, or culturally conditioned preferences, that determine our attitudes on such matters. Every speech-community seems to have its own prevalent ideas of "the beautiful", which often differ or are actually opposed from one language to another. Thus, in standard German the replacement of /s/ by /š/ before a consonant counts as "correct" and "elegant" (e.g. in *stehen* /šté:n/ "stand"), whereas in Italian the same replacement is quite "vulgar" and dialectal (especially Neapolitan, as in *stare* /štáre/ "stand"). The same considerations apply to morphology, syntax, and lexicon, for which the criteria of beauty and elegance differ not only from one community, but from one generation and one age to the next. For instance, the baroque convolutions of early seventeenth-century literary usage (parallel to those of the visual arts) seemed beautiful for a time, fell into disfavor for nearly three centuries, and in recent years have returned to favor. But some kind of artistically prestigious use

[37]

seems to many (perhaps even most) people a prime prerequisite for any variety of language to deserve respectful imitation.

The least personal of all the non-linguistic factors in idiolectal interaction is that of prescription, since it sets up standards which lay claim to unquestionable validity without reference to individual preference or reaction. The crassest type of prescription is the *ipse dixit*, in which the opinion or "say-so" of some one person is set up as an inflexible norm before which every speaker in the community must kow-tow, as was expected of the citizens of Uri in front of Gessler's hat set upon a pole. A slightly less personal type of prescription is that imposed by a more generalized belief in "correctness", whether imposed by a consensus of opinion within the community or by the fiat of some officially established body such as the French Academy. In many modern speech-communities which, through historical accident, never had an Academy (e.g. the English-speaking or the German-speaking world) other types of authority are appealed to, e.g. an artificially established stage-pronunciation (the "Bühnenaussprache") in Germany, or dictionaries and grammar-books in England, America, and the Commonwealth. It has been pointed out that we do not need any Academy to "regulate" the English language, since our secretaries, typists, copy-editors, and other people who are called on to deal with language-matters but are insecure in their knowledge of them, can find an apparently decisive answer in "the dictionary". Which dictionary?—it doesn't seem to matter very much, as long as it is "authoritative" and hence leaves no room for doubt or uncertainty. What such people want is to have every problem, even the slightest, solved in yes-or-no terms, and to have an unambiguous decision handed down from on high so as to relieve them of the responsibility of knowing the facts and reaching a decision on their own.

The penalty for any individual's not following the standards which others impose on him may vary from severe to light. Probably no-one was ever executed merely for using a "wrong" pronunciation or grammatical form, but physical punishment is often meted out, especially to children. I clearly remember being spanked and having my mouth washed out with soap and water for using "bad language", a not uncommon punishment for many children. In earlier times, adults as well were put in stocks or pillory for profanity. Negative sanctions can include more or less severe ostracism, and many a person has lost a job, a contract, or a possible spouse because of non-standard linguistic behavior. Pleasure, as well as displeasure, with a speaker's language can be conveyed to him by all kinds of informal means, from imperceptible nods or smiles to overt praise, especially in the case of children. Whether formal rewards, such as medals or prizes for success in writing poems, in oratory or in debating, are very effective in the moden English-speaking world, may be questioned (as may the effectiveness of marks in school). In other speech-communities, e.g. those of Spanish and Portuguese, such approbation is both sought after and effective in furnishing a model for imitation.

These are the channels through which the individual speaker is likely to have other individuals' pleasure or displeasure in linguistic matters conveyed to him, and the types of sanctions—positive and negative—which may be employed. As to the nature of linguistic norms themselves, there are at least eight major types, as distinguished by the Hungarian linguist Z. Gombocz. Here it will be enough to enumerate them and add a brief comment to each:

1. The literary norm, in which the usage of "the best authors" in a language is to serve as a model. It is always difficult or impossible to decide which authors are the best, especially when we descend below the level of the two or three top ones who are recognized as such by the entire community (e.g. Shakespeare, Milton; Lope de Vega, Cervantes). There is, furthermore, always a certain circularity in the process of determining what is "the language of the best authors". Who are the best authors?—those who use the best language. What is the

[39]

best language?—that used by the best authors. Furthermore, the "best" authors have a way of being much freer in their usage than the rules and regulations set up in their name by puristic language-legislators, as in the case of the double negative or the double superlative in Shakespeare (*the most unkindest cut of all*). At its most ridiculous, puristic criticism of literary usage leads self-appointed legislators to set up arbitrary rules which they then tell us "are violated by the very best authors in the language".

2. The historical norm, i.e. the usage of an earlier time, whether relatively recent or millennia earlier. This was a very common type of norm in the Renaissance, when, for Latin, Ciceronian style was widely prescribed, and similarly, for Italian, that of Petrarch in verse and Boccaccio in prose. In our day, the well-known "diglossia" of Modern Greek has arisen from an opposition between the *dhimotikí* or normal every-day usage, and the *katharévousa* or "purified" language, adapted as much as possible to the Periclean Greek of nearly 2500 years ago. The defenders of such a norm contend that they are upholding the "best" stage of a language, before which it was still imperfect and after which it has declined. This attitude rests on a faulty comparison of a language with an organism, considering it to be a living being with birth, youth, prime, decline, and old age. In actual fact, a language cannot be called an organism in any sense, since the distinguishing feature of an organism is that it has a life-cycle. A language is simply the ensemble of all the speaking- and writing-habits of the group that use it; it has no life-cycle, and no features that could be said to "improve" or "decay" from any objective point of view.

3. Popular speech, set up more or less in opposition to literary usage or to the language of the upper classes. In its most elementary manifestation, it involves deliberate use of forms like *ain't* or *he don't* in order to show the speaker's independence of

school-marms' prescriptions. (Since such a speaker is at the opposite pole from Miss Fidditch, the archetype of the fussy old-maidish purist, he has been called Mr. Chiddif.) A somewhat more extensive variety of this norm was at the base of Ivar Aasen's deliberate choice of contemporary Norwegian peasant speech for his *Landsmål*. Such an attitude was, in earlier times, an outgrowth of nineteenth-century Romanticism, which viewed the common folk and their ways as sounder, healthier, and purer than the aristocracy or the bourgeoisie. In more recent times, it has often been an expression of simple rebelliousness against the existing order. In either case, a less romantic view-point enables us to see that there is no particular merit in the behavior-patterns of any one social or geographical group, except that which we read into them on the basis of our own likes and dislikes.

4. Efficiency as a norm, prescribing the variety of language which is most efficient in conveying its user's meaning, with the least ambiguity and expenditure of effort. This norm might seem to appeal to modern times, with our emphasis on efficiency and avoidance of waste, and especially to logicians and mathematicians, who spend their time trying to construct artificial pseudo-languages which will embody just these characteristics. However, real language inevitably has to have redundancy built into it, to be usable in a wide range of circumstances; and it is, as has been pointed out, comparable to a low-energy control-system, in which only a very small amount of effort is used, at the most. Hence, for our use of real language (including that of literary prose or poetry), attempts to make it wholly logical or to save energy are not only beside the point, but quite harmful to its essence.

5. Authority, whether that of a Malherbe's or a school-marm's *ipse dixit*, an Academy's ruling, or a dictionary's listing. This ideal dates from the period of the "authoritarian reaction", the despotism of the Baroque period. Its main appeal, as a standard to follow, is to persons with a slave mentality, who are ready

[41]

or even wish to exchange their birth-right to independent action for the masochistic pleasure of subjecting themselves to the tyranny of others.

6. Logic—in this case, not the formal logic of philosophers, but the presumed "logic" inherent in the grammatical structure of some particular language. In the Renaissance, Latin was the favorite source of such logic, but, with the cultural and especially military dominance of France under Louis XIV and Louis XV, French took its place. Ever since Rivarol's notorious *Discours sur l'universalité de la langue française* (1784), it has been part of Western European folk-lore about language that French is especially clear and logical. On the contrary, French is neither more nor less logical than any other language. All languages are equally alogical, or, as Sapir put it, "all grammars leak". Hungarian may be illogical from the point of view of French in saying *három könyv* "three book" instead of *trois livres* "three books"; but French is equally illogical from the point of view of Hungarian, in needlessly insisting on an extra indication of the plural, already indicated once in the numeral. No kind of logic, whether the formal variety of the philosophers or the informal kind of the purist's arm-chair, can ever be relevant to linguistic structure, which has its own reasons for never remaining within any artificial constraints that might be dictated by abstract reasoning.

7. Geography, in the preference accorded to the speech of one region over that of another—e.g. London in England, Paris in France, Madrid in Spain, or Florence in Italy. Often, after the usage of a given locality has come to be regarded as standard, there are later developments in its popular speech which cause the latter to be regarded as vulgar ("cockney"), and the language of some near-by, usually smaller and more conservative locality is said to be "better" (e.g. Oxford, Orléans, Toledo, Siena). The norm thus set up is the chief kind of standard that speakers actually esteem and observe, as opposed to the artificial ones

[42]

which theoreticians defend in their elucubrations. But here again, taken in and for itself, the speech of, say, Paris is inherently neither better nor worse than that of Brussels, Geneva or Marseilles: Parisian is best for the Parisians, *Bruxellois* is best for the inhabitants of Brussels, etc. What causes people to think the speech of a given region superior to that of others is always some non-linguistic factor. The language of London, Paris, Madrid came to be regarded as standard because those cities were dominant politically and administratively; the dominance of Florence in Italy came about more through that city's economic supremacy. Obviously a capital city is more favored in this respect than others, and most of the geographically based standard languages of our times are indeed out-growths of the dialects of national or regional capitals.

8. Aesthetics—the supposed beauty of a given linguistic variety. Thus, we are often told that Tuscan Italian is more musical than any other language. This criterion is often used negatively, to condemn some language or dialect as "harsh", "guttural", or "unmusical". No competent linguist would take the aesthetic norm seriously any more, since it is so obviously dependent on personal preferences: beauty lies in the eye (in this case, the ear) of the beholder, and only there. Among the uninformed, however, it is still widely believed that beauty or the absence thereof can be an inherent characteristic of language; this notion is especially common in countries such as Italy, where the myth of the aesthetic absolute is still very much alive.

As Gombocz pointed out, these norms are usually invoked in dealing with literary usage, at least with regard to European standard languages. In modern times, however, with the extension of literacy to all or most of the population in many countries, the problem has come to affect much wider segments of the speech-community than formerly: glottopolitical problems arise such as the choice of language to be taught in the schools, used

[43]

in official activities and documents, or encouraged for bellettristic and journalistic writing. With newly established national languages (e.g. Hindi), the problem of the establishment of norms comes to be considered acute, although in many instances it is so only if one insists on a wholly unified, invariable standard. No responsible linguist would deny the existence of norms within speech-communities; on the other hand, insistence on presumably absolute or intrinsic norms can best be left to persons without any competence in linguistics, and it is the competent linguist's duty to disabuse such persons. All norms are relative and temporary, and all are derived from non-linguistic sources. Their usefulness lies only in aiding a new or insecure speech-community to attain a relative consensus of opinion and behavior on individual points that might other-wise cause difficulty (e.g. scientific terminology). In other contexts, the imposition of an absolute norm serves only to bolster the imposers' egos and to enable them to subjugate (even if only temporarily and partially) those other members of the speech-community who are willing to knuckle under.

In the light of these considerations, it is evident that the Saussurean distinction between *langue* and *parole*, if interpreted as that between community-imposed norm and individual realization thereof, is quite untenable. As we have just seen, the norms that are customarily proposed are related principally to the literary variety of a language, and are not usually expected to apply to every-day speech. If we wish to include the latter in an attempt to find a norm valid for all aspects of a community's linguistic activity, our resultant norm can only be a statistical one, representing the behavior of a numerical majority of the speakers. This remains true even if we attempt to weight our data in some way so as to take into account such factors as the social standing of some speakers. But a statistical norm can never be regarded as representing the usage of a community as a whole, even by the crassest principle of majority-rule. Add to this the fact that no collectivity exists apart from or outside of the individuals that make it up, as we saw in Chapter 1, and the entire notion, even the possibility, of a "collective norm" vanishes without leaving a trace, and therefore that of *langue* in the Saussurean sense does also. Individual behavior is not the partial manifestation of some Platonic ideal, inaccessible to scientific observation but evocable as the source of a norm to be imposed on every individual in the name of a collectivity. *La parole,* in the sense of actual speech-activity, is the only basis possible for our study and analysis of a non-Saussurean type of *langue,* the system of each idiolect.

We have had to take this long detour through the investigation of norms and their nature in order to clear the ground for a more profitable discussion of the relation of language to society and its function therein, freed from the distracting question of the imposition of norms. Language is customarily considered one of the major forces making for cohesion within human groups, and rightly so. As has been repeatedly pointed out, linguistic communication is a means whereby a stimulus originating in one person's brain can be transferred to the nervous and muscular system of one or more other persons—a transferral of which apparently no other living beings are capable in the same degree or with similar precision. Language is not a perfect means of communication, but it seems to be uniquely adapted to human needs—or perhaps, to a certain extent, the reverse may be true, that human needs have developed and been adapted in accordance with the messages that can be conveyed by language.

Human society depends for its very existence on the division of labor, carried far beyond biologically imposed necessities. Socially conditioned division of labor could never have come into existence without the prior existence and functioning of language. It has on occasion been maintained that language must have come into existence because of the division of labor. A minute's thought will show that both the type and the extent of communication required for the assignment of tasks and the coördination of even two individuals' activities are such that they presuppose at least the rudiments of an already developed communicative system.

[45]

This observation does not exclude the possibility that proto-hominids may have had other types of communicative systems (e.g. visual) before the oral-auditory type, with the duality of patterning which characterizes all known linguistic structures, came to be dominant.

The extent of coöperation possible within a non-literate speech-community is limited by the range of immediate (mostly, but by no means wholly, face-to-face) contacts which its members have with each other, and by their memories of what they have heard from members of the group, especially older persons—with the possibilities both of accurate transmission through memorization, and of gradual loss of accuracy through mis-hearing and mis-interpretation. The use of writing adds nothing brand-new to the nature of communication, but makes its spread far greater—in space, by enabling widely separated members to communicate more or less rapidly, and in time, by furnishing a semi-permanent record of most (not all) significant features of an utterance, which can then be transmitted unchanged over a relatively long period (as much as several millennia). Accuracy of transmission is also greatly increased by the use of writing, at least with regard to those linguistic features which it represents, though it also creates new difficulties with regard to possible ambiguities in its inter-pretation (especially with regard to intonation and other supra-segmental features). The degree of social coöperation and co-hesion made possible is thus greatly enhanced, as evidenced by the efforts of early priestly and aristocratic castes to keep the secret of writing to themselves.

Language can also serve as a means of social division, whereby one individual or group can be set against another. Dif-ferences in dialect often serve as pegs on which to hang all kinds of inimical action, from mere snobbery and social discrimination, all the way to the slaughter which the men of Gilead perpetrated on forty-two thousand Ephraimites because they said *sibboleth* instead of *shibboleth* (Judges 12.6). Even more serious, perhaps, is the possibility of deception furnished by two key properties of

linguistic structure: negation and displacement, so that it is possible for any-one to make not only true, but false statements about
phenomena not present in the immediate context, on which the
hearer cannot make an immediate check. Hence the entire range
of social disruption which is made possible through the lie—from
the child's fib, through his parents' "white lie" designed to make
a difficult situation easier, all the way to the extensive, systematic
falsehoods of Hitlerite or Communist propaganda.

The function of literature, i.e. art whose medium is language,
is partly individual and partly social. Of course, a work of literature is an expression of special perceptions of some kind on the
part of its author, and has its particular appeal (or lack thereof)
to each individual hearer or reader by virtue of his personal experience to which it does or does not seem to him to be related.
Whether the community elects to regard a literary work as valuable, and (as in one well-known definition of literature) to insist
on its repetition from time to time in substantially unchanged
form, is what determines its social function. In many, if not indeed most, societies the oral or written literature, as recited
aloud or studied in schools, is the means whereby cultural attitudes and ideals are handed down. When literature becomes the
property of exclusivist cliques and coteries, who set technique
above message and who transform literature into something eso-
teric and incomprehensible to the average individual, the culture
loses one of its most vital channels of transmission of its ideals. We
are witnessing the result of such a devaluation of literature in our
own times. The pressure of organized minority-groups with perse-
cution-complexes is depriving our school-children of such treas-
ures of our cultural heritage as Shakespeare's *Merchant of Venice*
and *Othello* and Mark Twain's *Huck Finn,* and cynical literary
critics' condemnation has spear-headed the drive for rejection of
many other valuable works of literature, especially of the Romantic period (e.g. Longfellow, Whittier, Bryant, Lowell in
America). Literary expression is only the "top of the ice-berg",
as the well-known metaphor has it, with respect to the totality of

[47]

human linguistic activity; but it is the top of the ice-berg which is immediately evident and hence attracts the most attention. Of all aspects of our linguistic behavior, it is literature which in many ways exerts the greatest immediate effect upon the ideals and mores of a society.

4

THE CHARACTERISTICS
OF LINGUISTIC STRUCTURE

That there is a structure in the linguistic behavior of every human, and that languages do constitute systems, has been recognized for a long time. If anything, in our century there has been an exaggeration of the systematic nature of linguistic structure, best exemplified in the definition of *la langue* which has been variously ascribed to Ferdinand de Saussure and to Antoine Meillet, as "le système où tout se tient". No, not everything: there are, in people's linguistic behavior, features which are not systematic. A given person may know a peculiar sound which does not fit into the normal phonological system of the speech-community as a whole, and may use this sound only in one word (e.g. /báx/ for *Bach*). He may have aberrant morphological or syntactic formations: one friend of mine uses the past tenses *arrove* for *arrived* and *subscrub* for *subscribed*—humorously, but none the less frequently. (We cannot leave humorous and playful linguistic behavior out of our consideration of language as a whole.) Such non-systematic features constitute a continually shifting border-zone on the fringes of systematic behavior. A "système où TOUT se tient" can exist only for the closed, no longer changing usage of the classical form of a dead language (e.g. Ancient Greek, Classical Latin, puristic literary French). It would have been much better to speak of "le système où PRESQUE TOUT se tient".

As we saw in the last chapter, the distinction between *langue* on the one hand and *parole* (or any synonym one chooses for the latter, such as *discours*) on the other, is quite fallacious. There exist only individual linguistic systems, manifested in the behavior and stored (as it would seem at present) in the brains of individual speakers. Another currently fashionable distinction, between COMPETENCE and PERFORMANCE, is basically valid, but we must make further distinctions within what is called "competence". The CAPACITY to use language is innate, species-specific, and is part of the more general capacity of humans to use symbols. It is well known, from experimental studies, that even apes are not able to use symbols in the same way, especially when displaced, i.e. when the thing symbolized is not present in the immediate context—as when, for example, a young chimpanzee being brought up in a human family was able to grasp the fact that the word "toidey" was used when the object itself was present; but when it was not present she looked around for it and, not seeing it, was greatly puzzled. Similarly, chimpanzees can apparently be taught to drive little automobiles, and to stop when a traffic-light changes from green to red; but, when the light goes red, they stop exactly where they are, and cannot be taught to continue going until they reach the light and then to stop there. In other words, the red light is purely a SIGN to stop, not a SYMBOL of a command "stop when you have come to this point." As a human grows and builds up his or her idiolect (cf. Chapter 2), we are witnessing the unfolding of the innate linguistic capacity which we all have as part of our genetic inheritance.

COMPETENCE, on the other hand, can refer only to the ability of an individual to use a given linguistic system, stored in his head, with its various structural characteristics and features of meaning. Which linguistic system an individual develops competence in, depends wholly on the accidents of personal history—

[50]

which speech-community he has been, not even born into, but brought up in; and, if the individual learns more than one language, it depends on which ones he has come in contact with. The degree of competence attained depends, obviously, on the models which the speaker has had for imitation, as sources for his knowledge. If a person brought up in the English-speaking world has never come across, for instance, the use of *do* as a pro-verb in the question-and-answer situation (*Have you written to Genevieve yet?—Oh, no; should I have done?*), or the use of the *-ing*-form as a passive participle (*There's a man here who has some French letters that he wants translating*), that person will never use those particular constructions, or even understand them without some confusion and difficulty.

An individual's PERFORMANCE is simply the manifestation, on a specific occasion, of selected features of the total set of linguistic abilities which he has stored up and on which he can draw as necessary. It is well known that in actual speech—not only very widely in every-day conversation, which goes on almost wholly outside of awareness so far as the selection of linguistic features is concerned, but even in ultra-careful, formal speech such as lectures, sermons, and orations—our performance is liable to all kinds of slips which may either pass unnoticed by both speaker and hearer, or else be corrected by the speaker either spontaneously or after it has been called to his attention by one or more listeners. Of course this implies that, inside each speaker's head, there exists a model (which we can call his competence) against which he can check his performance, and on the basis of which he can construct new, spur-of-the-moment analogies; blend already existing patterns in a previously unfamiliar way; and change what he has just said, replacing it by something closer to what he and/or his hearers might have expected. But this relationship between performance and competence does not justify us in regarding the latter as some kind of Platonic ideal of which the former is a pale, imperfect reflection, nor in considering that slips in performance must always be due to some

[51]

outside, non-linguistic factor which has impeded the speaker from giving a perfect realization of a pre-existing model. In the first place, the speaker's competence is never wholly organized into a system (and, as we have seen, each idiolect exists in and for itself, not as a manifestation of some over-all *langue* hovering like an invisible miasma over and determining the usage of the individual members of the speech-community). There are always gaps in each speaker's linguistic system; and, when a person speaks, his departures from what is customary may be due just as much to spur-of-the-moment analogy or to blending (e.g. when an adult uses forms like *mans* or *catched* wholly unintentionally) as to some kind of faulty actualization of a hypothetically perfect system.

Another widely-touted difference is that between "surface" and "deep" structure, or, going even farther, between these and "deeper" structure. It is asserted in some quarters that what we have traditionally, as linguists, for the last one and two-thirds centuries, been concerned with analyzing, and whose differences we have done our best to observe and formulate, is merely "surface" structure; that there is a "deep" structure underlying this "surface" structure, which is aprioristically declared to be the same for all human language; and that what we ought to be doing is, not wasting our time on studying the differences between surface structures, but seeking to discover and explicate the features common to all human use of language, as manifested in deep (deeper, deepest) structure. The use of the terms *surface* and *deep* (and especially of the adjective *superficial*) constitutes, in this connection, a covert appeal to emotional prejudices associated, in our society, with these terms. They have a widespread connotation, the former unfavorable and negative (implying failure to penetrate to some inner essence), and the latter favorable and positive. All one needs to do, to play on one's audience's secondary emotional associations, is to attach labels of this kind to phenomena and then to use them in contexts which will cause one's hearers or readers to have negative or positive

[52]

reactions. What is usually labelled "deep" structure is, in fact, nothing but a paraphrase of a given construction, concocted *ad hoc* to enable the grammarian to derive the latter from the former by one kind of manipulation or another. Thus, we may decide that the verb *to gate-crash* has the deep structure *to crash the* (or *a*) *gate*. Why not *to crash through the* (or *a*) *gate?*—because the former is easier to perform grammatical operations on. In clause-structure, the syntactic kernel of the subject-plus-predicate construction is said to be the deep structure of the sentence; and if an utterance cannot be reduced to a subject-plus-predicate kernel, it is denied the charismatic label of "well-formed sentence". When it comes to other languages than English, their deep structure always turns out to be that of English; in other words, we are now witnessing the forcing of all languages into the mould of English, just as in earlier periods they were forced into that of Classical Latin. "Deeper" structures turn out to be simply the meaning of utterances.

We shall discuss in the next chapter the import of the notions of "deep" and "deeper" structure for our techniques of linguistic analysis. Here, it will be enough to say that the distinction between "surface" structure and any degree of "depth" is wholly unjustified, at least in the sense in which these terms have been used in transformational-generative speculations. There is simply linguistic structure, i.e. the patterns which people follow in talking to each other and in reacting to what they hear from others (including, of course, different levels or planes of organization inherent in the structure itself), and there are the meanings of these patterns, i.e. the correlations between them and the environment in which they are used (including correlations with other linguistic patterns, or "grammatical meaning"). Linguistic structures do differ, very widely indeed, among all the attested languages of the earth, and so do the semantic relationships which are associated with linguistic structures. The search for linguistic universals—features common to all languages—after being nearly tabooed for a century or more, has recently come to the fore again, but it is still premature to expect that we can make any except the most elementary observations concerning linguistic universals and expect them to be permanently valid. Our knowledge of two-thirds or more of the world's languages is still too scanty (or, in many instances, non-existent); nor is abstract speculation, on an *a priori* rationalistic basis, any valid substitute for conclusions based on direct observation or controlled extrapolations therefrom, and testing of the hypotheses thus established.

The two basic planes on which humans behave in their linguistic activity are those of PHONOLOGY and MORPHOLOGY-SYNTAX (or TACTICS). These are usually referred to as *levels*, and often the relationships between them are indicated in diagrams such as the following:

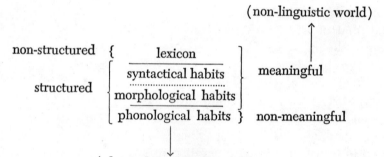

Such a diagram can be very useful in showing how, by means of a system with a relatively complex organization, there is a connection between the physical sounds of speech and the non-linguistic world. We must be careful, however, to avoid the implications of hierarchical value which our culture seems almost inevitably to attach to the upper-vs.-lower dimension of such a representation. Just because, in a two-dimensional diagram, the lexicon and syntactical habits are placed above the morphological, and all of these above the phonological, does not justify us in concluding either that the former are more important than the

[54]

latter, or vice-versa. In the actual use of language, the speaker is engaging in activity on all these "levels" at once, and the hearer is responding to all at the same time. For one type of description or another, it may be more convenient to start at the "bottom" or at the "top"; but this is a matter of analytical or didactic convenience, not of any supposed inherent importance of one plane or level over another in the structure itself.

Because morphologico-syntactic habits are both patterned and meaningful, they are usually considered to form the central core of linguistic structure, so that lexicon as such is often neglected, and some theorists would exclude not only the physical sounds of speech, but all considerations of phonology, from linguistics. Neither of these exclusions is justified. The lexicon of a language is the chief means whereby both denotational and connotational meanings are conveyed, and its phonology is the only means whereby forms, constructions, and lexical items (i.e. all the rest of the structure) are made in any wise perceptible.[1] The fundamental division between phonology and tactics does indeed imply duality in structure, what has rightly been termed "la double articulation du langage"; but duality in structure does not justify the assumption of dualism, in the traditional Platonic sense. It is not valid to consider the phonic actuality of speech to be "merely the physical manifestation of a pre-existing psychic reality" and hence to dismiss phonology from our consideration. Nor are we entitled to do so because deaf-mutes and people handicapped by one type or another of brain-injury are able (often, but not always) to find substitutes for part or even all of the phonological system. Similar development of substitutes for missing or defective capacities is well known for many other

1. I am considering to be self-evident the fact that writing is not co-equal with sound as an embodiment of linguistic form and structure, but is, in all its functioning in connection with real language, simply a derivative of this latter, representing, normally, one aspect or another of phonology, or else (as in the case of Chinese characters) of features of morphology.

aspects of human behavior, without invalidating the basic importance of those aspects in normal people's life. For normal human beings, in normal social contact, the sounds of their language, and intercourse by means of speaking and hearing, are and have been for countless millennia, a fundamental part of their linguistic activity, which should not be denied or pushed aside.

It is not wise, however, to regard the various levels or planes of linguistic structure as absolutely water-tight compartments, with no relation between each other. There are ways in which, for instance, features of phonology indicate boundaries between morphological units, in phenomena of juncture (which act, therefore, as "Grenzsignale" or boundary-markers, in the terminology of the Prague school)—for example, the well-known distinction in English (optional, but available to every speaker if he wants to make it) between /ə+ném/ *a name* and /ən+ém/ *an aim*. For a certain time, in some quarters, it was rank heresy to admit that there could be such interrelations. We must recognize that they do exist, and that there is no justification for denying their existence. On the other hand, it is equally unjustified to deny that there are various levels of linguistic structure, with fundamentally different characteristics, even though the boundaries between them may, at certain points, be difficult to determine, and though overlapping may take place.

Like all structures, that of language is made up of significant units. To deny the existence of such units in language would be like denying that of atoms in the structure of matter (even though, in both cases, it is possible to go below the level of the single unit). The oft-made distinction between "emic" and "etic" is highly useful here, with the latter referring to any feature of behavior viewed as raw material, without regard to its function in contrast with other features of behavior, and the former referring to significant units. What is significant on one level of structure may of course be simply an element of raw material and hence etic on another. Thus, a course (soup, fish, entrée, dessert) is an emic unit in the structure of a single meal, but in the context of a whole day's dietemic behavior, it is the meals themselves which are the emic units and the courses of which they are made up are simply raw material, relative to the day's behavior as a whole. Similarly, in linguistic structure, an individual sound is an etic element within the phonemic unit of which it forms part; but that phoneme and the other phonemic units in the phonological system are, in their turn, simply the "building-blocks", as it were, of which the morphemes of the language consist.

From what we have just said, it is obvious that we must recognize the existence of significant units on the various levels or planes of linguistic structure. There exists a widely used set of terms, formed on Greek roots by suffixing *-eme* to refer to significant units, and by prefixing *allo-* for the non-significant variants:

GREEK ROOT	SIGNIFICANT UNIT	NON-SIGNIFICANT VARIANT
phon- "sound"	phoneme	allophone
ton- "pitch"	toneme	allotone
morph- "form"	morpheme	allomorph
tagm(a) "arrangement"	tagmeme	allotagma
lex- "word"	lexeme	allolex
graph- "phonemic shape"	grapheme	allograph
sem- "meaning" etc.	sememe	alloseme

For some of the emic and etic units thus set up, it will be easier to define their boundaries than for others; for sememes and allosemes, especially, it is (as we shall see later in this chapter) impossible, in our present state of knowledge of the universe, to establish sharp limits to the range of each item we treat. We must also recognize that, on many occasions, units whose basic function is on one level (e.g. clauses, phrases, morphemes) can shift their rank and be used in other functions in further combinations: e.g. the clause *I saw* when it is rank-shifted and used as a modifier in a noun-phrase, such as *the man I saw* (optionally expandable to *the man whom I saw*); or the modal verb *might* shifted to the function of a main verb in the following dialogue, which I heard the night before this page was written:

A. Being absent from a concert without a valid written excuse might lead to expulsion from the Glee Club.
B. It doesn't might; it does.

In connection with the existence of various, fundamentally different levels, it is well to recall the distinction—essential to all linguistic analysis—between free and bound forms. In all Indo-European languages and in (it is probably safe to say) most others, some forms can occur alone, and others are restricted to occurrence only together with other forms, as in the well-known instances of suffixes like the English verb-endings spelled *-ing*, *-(e)s, -ed;* the comparative and superlative endings *-er* and *-est;* the noun-plural-suffix in its various allomorphs; a host of prefixes such as *pre-, ab-, ad-, ex-;* and so on ad infinitum. In some instances, an emic unit may have some etic variants which are free and others bound, as in the pronoun-systems of the Romance languages. Thus, French has a first-person-singular pronoun, with a free or "disjunctive" allomorph *moi,* and two bound or "conjunctive" allomorphs, *je* (subject) and *me* (direct and indirect object). Hypostasis (treating bound forms as free, as in Bloomfield's well-known example of "a girl in her *teens,* taking up all kinds of *isms* and *ologies*", or a man referring to his former wife as "my *ex*") is a border-line-case, another instance of rank-shifting, which does not invalidate the fundamental distinction between free and bound forms. Bondage is most noticeable, and hence has been traditionally recognized most easily, on the morphological level, in inflection and derivation. It is essential to realize, however, that it can also occur on all syntactic levels, and on that of lexical combination as well. Such forms as the English indefinite article *a, an;* the definite article *the;* and the possessive suffix spelled *'s*, are all PHRASALLY bound. Similarly, the Haitian Creole negativizer *pa-* "not" comes only before predicates, and is therefore PREDICATIVELY bound; and our conjunctions *that, if, although,* etc., are CLAUSALLY bound. Certain lexical items occur only in fixed combinations, e.g. *kith* (used, in standard English, only in *kith and kin*) or *let* "impediment" (occurring only in *without let or hindrance*); these are LEXICALLY bound. Languages can of course differ tremendously in the extent to which their elements are free or bound, and there may even be languages in which there are no bound elements at all. Even if there were such, however, this would not invalidate the distinction and its importance and usefulness.

Certainly, if we recognize the existence of bondage on all levels of grammatical structure, the necessity of considering the "word" as a linguistic universal disappears. Much of the extensive argument over the word and its nature has arisen because the discussion has been couched in terms of orthography; but the spelling of many (especially European) languages calls for spaces between, not only free forms, but also phrasally and clausally bound forms (*an apple,* not **anapple; the book,* not **thebook*). Hence many forms traditionally termed "words", such as our articles and most (not all) of our prepositions and conjunctions, are thereby misclassified and the debate has been based on inaccurate data. In some languages, such as French, the proportion of bound forms to free is much higher than might be thought on the basis of their orthographical representation. For instance, in such a French sentence as that written *je ne lui en ai pas encore donné* "I haven't given him any of it yet", we recognize eight separate words in its orthographical representation. But as spoken, it is /žən(ə)lüiãne^pazãkordone^/, a single phonological group, containing five phrasally bound elements (/žə/ "I", /nə/ and /paz/ "not", /lüi/ "to him" and /ãn/ "of it"), two inflectionally bound (/e^/ "have" and /don-/ "give"),[2] and one

2. By some systems of analysis, the elements /e^/ "(I) have" and /done^/ "given" might be counted as containing several morphemes, of

inflectionally bound (/-e^/ past participle ending); there is only one free form which could count as a "word" by criteria of freedom and bondage, /ākor/ "yet".

One of the major developments of twentieth-century linguistics has been the recognition that not only difference, but CONTRAST between elements is a fundamental principle in the organization of language-structure. It is not enough to observe that two items differ from each other in one way or another (for a consonant, for instance, with regard to aspiration). For the difference between two items to have functional significance in a system, they must contrast with each other; otherwise the difference is not significant. (The classical example is the absence of contrast between aspirated and unaspirated stop-consonants [p t k b d g] in English, as opposed to the presence of contrast between voiced and voiceless consonants, e.g. [p] vs. [b] in such pairs as *pit* and *bit*.) A very frequent type of contrast is that in which one item has a specific feature (is "marked", or, in the German expression used by the Prague school, is "merkmalhaft"), as opposed to the other, which simply does not have or is not limited to that specific feature (is "unmarked" or "merkmallos"). The English progressive verb-phrase (*is working, is coming*) is marked in that it has the meaning of "temporary" (with respect to the validity of the predication of the verb), as opposed to the simple form (*works, comes*), which is not marked in this respect and is not limited to "temporary" meaning, but can have either temporary or other types of meaning (generic, habitual, etc.).

The distinction between marked and unmarked can be extended to all levels of structure, including the lexical. Thus, in current American English, there are several terms referring to persons of African origin, but only one of these terms is marked for over-tones of courtesy (*Negro*, pronounced /níjgròw/ and spelled with capital *N*), whereas the others (e.g. the same

which some of the allomorphs might be treated as zero; but my point here is that each of these elements has at least one bound morpheme, if not more.

morpheme spelled with a lower-case *n*, or pronounced as /níjgrə/ or /nígrə/; the variant of that morpheme pronounced /nígər/ and spelled *nigger;* other words such as *darky,* etc.) are widely regarded as not only non-courteous but offensive. We must always recognize, however, that when contrast is absent, the differences in meaning which it conveys are also absent. Thus, in Mark Twain's *The Adventures of Huckleberry Finn,* the only word that Huck knows for persons of African origin is *nigger,* and hence it is the only term he uses throughout the book; but, by this same token, in Huck Finn the word *nigger* has no over-tones of discourtesy such as it is presumed to have by people who know other, competing forms. It was therefore a highly unperceptive action on the part of some civil-rights-advocates, with more idealism than knowledge of linguistic structure, to object to the presence of the word *nigger* in that book and therefore to call for its exclusion from libraries, whereas Twain's *Huck Finn* is actually the best pro-Negro book that has ever been written in the United States.

It must not be thought, however, that any one specific type of contrast is the only kind found in linguistic (or other) structure. In some quarters, it is thought that all contrasts can and should be reduced to two-way (binary) oppositions, with a yes-no type of answer to whatever question is asked concerning any given point in a net-work of contrasts. This type of binary opposition is indeed necessary for certain types of machines which work on an all-or-none principle, but is by no means a universal requirement for all contrast. As we have just seen, many contrasts, especially those of the "marked" vs. "non-marked" variety, can usefully be phrased in yes-no terms; but in some instances, the contrast clearly involves three or more co-equal terms. Thus, in some vowel-systems (e.g. French, German) there are three types of phonemes: front-unrounded, front-rounded, back-rounded (/i/ ~ /y/ ~ /u/; /e/ ~ /œ/ ~ /o/); and in some (e.g. Turkish) there are these three, plus a fourth (back-unrounded). Any combination of three items in contrast can of course be artificially reduced to two-plus-one or one-plus-two, and any combination of four items can similarly be artificially formulated as two-plus-two; but there is no reason inherent in the vowel-pattern of French or German itself why we should put the front-rounded series with the front-rounded as opposed to the back-rounded, or any reason in Turkish for putting the four series into two binary sub-groups. Contrast, in other words, can have more dimensions than just the two which are suggested by our bidimensional spatial representations in diagrams on paper or black-board.

On the phonological level, as suggested by our diagram on p. 54, the emic units have, in and for themselves, no correlation with any feature of the world in which we live: I would not normally go up to any-one and say /v/ or /í/ and expect to get any reaction (except perhaps "Waddaya mean by that?").[3] On other levels, however, each emic unit has, by definition, some type of correlation with some feature of the surrounding world (for if it did not have meaning, it would not be emic). Morphemes (free or bound), syntactic combinations, all are meaningful, each in its own right. Meaning is not something either wholly alien to linguistic structure (as a few misguided linguists tried to maintain for a time) or separable therefrom as an independent "semantic component" that can be peeled off and treated atomistically as if it were irrelevant to the grammatical system (as in the formulation "grammatical component + semantic component = linguistic structure"). The latter notion is really only a reformulation of the former, in currently more fashionable terms.

That meaning is the bridge between the sounds and forms of language, on the one side, and the facts of the universe in

3. There are of course instances of morphemes which consist of single phonemes, e.g. Eng. /ûw/ *ooh!* or /š/ *sh!,* or Fr. /o/ *eau* "water". From the point of view of the structure of the morphemes, however, the number of phonemes of which they consist is accidental, the result of historical happenstance.

[62]

which we live, on the other, has been recognized for a long time; but the exact way in which it is related to both sides has been the object of a great deal of (often quite futile) discussion. It is useful to distinguish clearly between linguistic forms and their combinations themselves, and their REFERENTS, i.e. the phenomena to which they refer. The meaning of a linguistic form is of course not the referent itself, but rather the correlation between the form and the referent in connection with which it occurs. This correlation is both positive and negative: a form has a given meaning insofar as it does occur in connection with a given referent, and does not have that meaning insofar as it does not occur in connection therewith. As a child is learning to speak, we say that he has learned the meaning of a form or construction if he correlates it with the same referent as do the speakers around him, and not until then. Jespersen tells of one child who failed to distinguish between "sing", "tell a story", and "play a game" for the word *sing,* and another who used *can't* for both "can't" and "won't". In the first case, the child's meaning for *sing* was simply "to play a game in which his elders amused him", and in the second, *can't* indicated refusal to do what she did not want to do.

Now a correlation can be of the all-or-none variety, or it can also involve gradience, with a rheostat-like variation from 100% to zero. In the case of meaning, we are dealing with the latter type of correlation. In ordinary language-use, we do not normally have sharp, clearly defined boundaries for the meanings of our linguistic forms. For even such common terms as *chair, salad, book, work* (to say nothing of color-names like *blue* and *green*) every one of us can think of border-line-cases in which it would be hard for us to decide definitively whether we would or would not use a given term. Is a tabouret a chair? Can a salad be a salad without lettuce? Is a "comic" a book? And every man has had arguments with his wife over whether a given dress is blue or green. These differences exist, not only from one individual to another, but within each individual's usage. On some occasions I

[63]

may fluctuate between thinking that writing a book is work and considering it play, or between calling a color blue and calling it green. This inherent, inevitable gradience and absence of sharp lines of demarcation in the correlation between linguistic forms and their referents is one of the reasons why it is impossible to establish clearly defined etic features of meaning (allosemes) and hence emic units of meaning (sememes) with the same type of precision that is possible with the forms and their combinations when considered by themselves.

As with every other aspect of linguistic structure, meaning is a purely individual, idiolectal phenomenon. When a person uses a feature of his or her idiolect, that feature is correlated with the entire surrounding circumstances of the phenomenon in connection with which it is used—not only, therefore, with the referent itself, but also with what is going on inside the speaker's entire system at the time; what has gone on inside the speaker on previous occasions in connection with the referent involved; and circumstances in the out-side world attendant on the use of the form, every time the speaker uses or has used it. These aspects of meaning are, of course, part of their CONNOTATION, as opposed to their DENOTATION or "dictionary-meaning". In certain types of discourse (scientific, mathematical, logical) it is considered desirable to minimize the connotational aspects of meaning; but they are an ineradicable part of normal people's use of real language in every-day living (which is, after all, its basic function in human existence), and we cannot push them out of the picture when considering language as a whole.

Again as with other facets of language, we can arrive at the meaning of a linguistic form for a speech-community only by a process of abstraction, omitting from our consideration those features (particularly the connotational) which are not common to all members of the group involved. Here, too, we must avoid hypostatizing and then reifying the abstractions we thus obtain. For many centuries, philosophers and lexicographers (and, in their wake, purists and language-reformers) have concluded, on the basis of such reification, that words have "true" or "real" meanings, any departure from which involves a "corruption" of the words' value and hence usefulness. (This attitude is at the base of the pronouncements of such authors as George Orwell or James Thurber on matters of language.) But the real meaning of any linguistic form or construction resides only in the actual correlation that each individual speaker makes between the form and the totality of the situation (as described in the previous paragraph) in which he or she uses it. Since we do not have at present—and do not seem likely to have in any foreseeable future —any means of finding out the state of any person's whole organism, either at a particular time or over a period of time, nor yet of discovering and describing the totality of any single occurrence in our world, it would seem quite hopeless to try to define meaning with any completeness. This consideration is at the base of the attitude that meaning is less amenable to scientific treatment than other parts of language-structure (see Chapter 5). Such an attitude, although quite valid, does not justify us in denying the existence or the relevance of meaning in language. The linguist can attain at least as much accuracy in defining and handling meaning as does the native speaker, who reaches an approximation of understanding on the basis of repeated observation—almost wholly outside of awareness—of the situations in which a form is used; and the linguist's analytical techniques should enable him to achieve a clearer overt formulation than the native speaker can usually make.

Every meaning inevitably involves abstraction, i.e. the selection of one or more features out of the totality of characteristics inherent in any phenomenon, or common to two or more phenomena, and the neglect of the rest. The ability of humans to make abstractions, and to symbolize them by means of linguistic forms, is at the very root of our use of language. Abstractions certainly exist; but the *locus existendi* of every abstraction is only inside the head of the person who makes it. Unreflecting speakers make their abstractions on the basis of their experience (in-

[65]

cluding what other people tell them, especially when they are children), and then think that their own abstractions are identical with those of all other speakers in their community. Roughly correspondent, yes; identical, no. Complete identity of abstractions (and hence of meanings) from one speaker to the next can be obtained only through identity of analytical procedures; the initial aim of any scientific analysis is just this—to set up clear, unambiguous definitions of terms and procedures of observation and formulation, so as to avoid the endless, futile debates that arise from divergent abstractions made by different observers in uncontrolled fashion. But such complete identity is attained only at the price of schematization, i.e. neglect of features considered to be subsidiary or unimportant in the phenomenon being studied. The greater the abstraction, the more of reality is neglected. Hence the inevitable and perennial tension between the partisans of abstraction (whose ultimate aberration, as we saw on p. 9, is idealism) and those of close observance of reality (who, if they refuse to make sufficient abstractions, fall into the opposite, though ultimately less damaging, error of empiricism). In both every-day life and scientific enquiry, abstraction is an essential part of the use of language, but is valid only insofar as it is ultimately tied to observable reality.

The reality or otherwise of the referent is quite irrelevant to the meaning of a word or other linguistic form, including a complete utterance with any kind of structure. Any combination of features in the real world, or in an imaginary world (e.g. those of science fiction) can serve as referent. This is what enables us to talk about phenomena which are mythical (unicorns, hippogriffs), not available to direct observation (electrons, protons), or unverifiable (angels, devils). As we saw earlier, it is the combination of displaced speech and negation which makes it possible for a lie to be told, without there being any way of finding, from the linguistic (phonological, grammatical, semantic) structure of the lying utterance, whether it is true or not. What is obviously true of a lie is also true of any other utterance, namely

[66]

that its truth must be discovered by verification of the facts involved. Since the facts themselves, and our view of them, can change, the truth of an utterance can likewise change, so that a statement which is false at one time can be true at another, and vice versa. It follows that the efforts of philosophers to examine "propositions" (which are simply a limited variety of utterances) to discover their truth-values on the basis of their linguistic structure are fore-doomed to failure.

Form and meaning, therefore, go together in the structure of language; neither one can be considered to be the "essence" of language in the absence of the other. However, since linguistic form is more easily observable, definable, and analyzable into significant units, it is from this side that our examination and formulation of language-structure should start. The details of our procedure in linguistic analysis will be taken up in the next chapter.

5

THE DESCRIPTION
OF LINGUISTIC STRUCTURE

We have seen (pp. 15–16) that a purely synchronic description of any phenomenon rests on a fiction, assuming unrealistically that no change takes place in the subject-matter while it is being observed and described. Such a fiction is, however, useful as long as we recognize it as such, and we shall maintain it throughout this chapter. How, then, are we to set about describing the structure of a linguistic system, as if it were an entity at a given point of time, and in a scientific manner?

On p. 14, we observed that the work of discovery is an essential part of scientific activity. No geologist, botanist, or zoölogist, say, would ever consider either his methods of gathering data or his work in examining and classifying them to be less scientific than the aim of formulating his results and relating them to the structure and history of the rest of the universe. Formulation, divorced from data-gathering and classification, is inherently exposed to the risk of becoming empty jugglery, in harmful imitation of mathematics and logic. For the linguist, the source of his data is important, and must be carefully checked on, because not all sources are equally trustworthy (and none is inherently or permanently so). Every human learns his native tongue through observation and imitation of others around him, arriving at a very close approximation of the usage of the rest of the community (never at a complete identity therewith—this would be, in the nature of things, impossible). This is a completely valid way for the linguist to approach his material, too, if he is dealing with a language that is not native to him. Every learner of a second language inevitably suffers a blockage resulting from the interference of his native linguistic structure, but a properly trained linguist can overcome this in himself. The time normally involved in acquiring a new language can be materially shortened by appropriate techniques of elicitation and study, even while the investigation is going on.

Of course there are limitations on the procedure of eliciting texts from informants, even when it is done by the most skilled linguist and the most sophisticated informant. Unless he has a very extensive corpus of material at his disposal—such as a large body of texts gathered over many years, or all the works of a great literature—there is always the risk that the linguist will fail to obtain some form or construction that may be crucial to some part of his analysis. (This happened to me, for instance, with Haitian Creole, when I mistakenly put /ānu/ "let's go, let's . . ." in the class of aspectival verb-prefixes, and found out only later that it can also occur as a free form.) However, the linguist is in exactly the same position, in this respect, as the native speaker, who may not have in his own idiolect some feature that other speakers have, and, if he has not met it, will not know it or be able to furnish it to the linguist (or to himself if he is his own linguist). It was not until the age of about forty that I came across the English construction *Here's somebody who has some letters in French that he wants translating* (p. 51), in which the -ing-form has passive meaning. This construction is used chiefly in the Midlands in England; it was quite foreign to me as a speaker of American English. Yet it is this construction which makes clear such expressions as *Here are some letters that want translating* ("need to be translated") or *There are a lot of old magazines kicking around in the attic* ("being kicked around").

[70]

In this situation, the most that the linguist can do is to gather and work on just as much material as he possibly can, until he reaches a point, not only of "diminishing returns", but at which the added increment of knowledge from further material becomes asymptotic to zero. In some instances, limitations on time, energy, or funds make such a procedure impossible, especially for investigators working on languages of "primitive" groups under difficult field-conditions. In such cases, we shall have to be content with the limited knowledge thus gained, recognizing that even a tenth of a loaf is better than none. There is no excuse for taking a patronizing or condescending attitude towards the hard-won information gained by "anthropological linguists", which is the only source that we shall ever have for cross-linguistic investigation.

Some investigators of language—especially those who believe in the existence of "deep structure" as a language-universal and its identity throughout the languages of the earth (p. 52)—have grown impatient with the delay in gathering information and with the incompleteness which inevitably results from the situation described in the previous paragraph, and will presumably be with us forever. This impatience has led to an attempt to find a short-cut, in the assumption that there is no need, or even that it is undesirable, to obtain material for analysis from native speakers of any language other than that of the investigator. It has been seriously maintained that no-one but a native speaker of a given language can ever investigate the "deep" (deeper, deepest, most deepest . . .) structure thereof, since only the native speaker can give a definitive decision as to whether a given feature is permissible ("grammatical", "correct", "acceptable", etc.) or not. However, we get around this difficulty by assuming (*a priori*, without demonstration) that the "deep structure" of all languages is identical. So, we are told, all we need to do is to discover it by looking into ourselves; asking ourselves questions as to what is grammatical and what is ungrammatical; and basing our analysis on what we know about our own language (English, of course, since most of those who take this position are speakers of English). A moment's reflection will show how misleading such a procedure, or any procedure of *a priori* rationalistic analysis which tries to deal with humans and their doings without taking culture into account, is bound to be. We have already pointed out (p. 8) that the notion of grammaticality is just the old doctrine of correctness—historically speaking, a relic of seventeenth- and eighteenth-century absolutism and authoritarianism—masquerading under a new name. Whether a linguistic phenomenon is "grammatical", "correct" or not depends only on the attitude of the speech-community towards it. If a speaker tells us that a given form or construction is or is not "grammatical", he is only reflecting (normally outside of awareness) the promptings of his linguistic super-ego (p. 25).

Grammaticality is, in any case, not a phenomenon that can be measured in terms of a simple binary opposition, declaring any linguistic phenomenon to be either grammatical or ungrammatical. There is an infinite gradation between something which every member of a speech-community would use and recognize unhesitatingly as completely normal, to the opposite extreme of something that every speaker would declare was never used. In between come all the possibilities of features which some people do use normally and others do not; of those which may occur sporadically in the usage of most or all of the members of the community; or of those which occur only infrequently (either because they are obsolete or because they have only recently arisen) but are understood by some, most, or all of the community. Furthermore, new formations resulting from analogy or blending are taking place all the time, and are being recognized and understood without difficulty. (To deny the validity or relevance of empirical evidence in this connection, as some have done, is to place one's assertions concerning grammaticality beyond the pale of scientific endeavor.) Some linguists, in an effort to make their formulations water-tight, have resorted to the notion of a "well-formed" sentence, one whose structure is wholly

[72]

grammatical, and have restricted their aim to providing formulas that can generate only well-formed sentences. The very notion of a contrast between "well-formed" and "ill-formed" sentences is, however, nothing but a recrudescence of the old contrast between "correct" and "incorrect"; there is no *a priori* criterion of logicality or rationality that can determine grammaticality or well-formedness for us. A naïve native speaker determines what seems normal or abnormal only on the basis of his own observation (with help, of course, from his linguistic super-ego, and wholly outside of awareness) of what is frequent and what is infrequent. The notion of a "well-formed" sentence can have validity only for a dead language, which is no longer used as the first language of a speech-community and hence is no longer subject to change. Any description of a living language, to be complete, must allow for open-endedness in the behavior of the speakers, and for departure from pre-existing patterns as well as obedience to them.

For that matter, what any speaker (even the most sophisticated linguist using himself as informant) may tell us concerning, not only grammaticality, but the actual facts of his own language, is always suspect. That introspection is a highly untrustworthy source of information, has been well known to doctors and psychologists for a long time. A person's knowledge concerning his own behavior is almost always incomplete and often inaccurate. The late W. D. Elcock tells of a highly typical occurrence: his informant in a village in Upper Aragon (Spain) had denied that either he or any-one else in the community ever used forms like /kadútu/ "fallen"; not over ten minutes later some-one else came in from out-side and used that very form in casual conversation with members of his family. Naïve speakers' awareness of what either they or others say is at best shadowy; when they attempt to introspect, they are likely to dredge up, not more accurate observations, but more confused and inaccurate impressions. The linguist trying to introspect is open to even greater dangers. In his attempt to discover confirmation for some theory, he is likely to invent artificial usages that are not actually typical of his

[73]

normal language-activity, or to distort his report on the frequency or importance of some linguistic feature, or (just like the most naïve speaker) to deny that he does something that he actually does. This last type of error in reporting one's own behavior is particularly likely to occur when an infrequent, but none the less real, phenomenon contradicts some pet theory. I have known linguists to deny the existence, in their own usage, of such English words as *dinghy* /díɲi/ or *hangar* /háeŋàr/, or of proparoxytone stress in such Italian words as *màndorla* "almond" or *pòlizza* "(insurance) policy", so as not to be compelled thereby to give up their formulations (in these instances, of the morphophonemic status of /ŋ/ in English and of stress in Italian, respectively).

It is clearly impossible to expect that we shall ever be able to train at least one native speaker of every language on earth (including all the aboriginal languages still spoken) to do linguistic analysis (of whatever variety) and to introspect sufficiently—even granting that this were a valid procedure—to give us a description of his own tongue. If we were to wait long enough for such training to be done, a large proportion (probably more than half, at the very least) of the world's languages, particularly the more obscure and "unusual" from our point of view, would disappear before even the slightest attempt could be made to record them. It is more important to get as much data, on as many languages and their structure and semantics, as possible, than it is to restrict our attestations to material formulated according to any particular system deemed by some the only "correct" approach.

Once we have gathered our material, we must analyze and formulate it. Ever since the Greek and Latin grammarians, it has been traditional to phrase linguistic data in terms of rules and exceptions: "An adjective must agree with its noun in gender, number, and case"; "The object of a verb must be in the accusative, except with five verbs (*utor, fruor, fungor, potior* and *vescor*) which take the ablative and with certain verbs which take the genitive (*meminor, obliviscor, recordor, reminiscor* and certain impersonals)." Since the use of rules and exceptions has been characteristic of prescriptive, normative grammars, there has been in the present century a determined effort to free linguistics from formulations involving rules, and to use objective, descriptive statements instead. Recently, as part of a general reaction in favor of apriorism, rationalism, absolutism, and authoritarianism in seventeenth-century style, there has been a return to the use of rules. We have been repeatedly told that a grammar should be "a set of ordered rules which will enable the grammarian to generate all the well-formed sentences of the surface-structure of a language from its deep structure, and no other sentences." How limited and inadequate such an aim is, should be evident to the reader who has followed us thus far. The much-belabored contrasts between surface and deep structure, and between well-formed and ill-formed sentences, are non-existent. There exist only structure and its associated meanings; there exist utterances of all kinds, statistically normal and not so normal. That there should be order in the statements we make concerning a language, is obvious; but this order should reflect the order which is inherent in the actual facts of the language itself, not that of some invented, arbitrarily imposed "logic" external to the language we are describing (whether the grammar of some other language, or a non-existent "universal logic" or "reason").

Our statements concerning a language should deal with actual language-data and their relations to each other, not imaginary intermediate steps concocted in order to form a bridge between one phenomenon and another. A recent transformational-generative statement concerning French possessive phrases sets up a series of stages to derive them from "propositions" concerning possession: thus, for *mon livre* "my book", we start from *le livre est à moi* "the book is to me = is mine" → *le livre à moi* "the book to me" → *DETERMINER + livre + PRONOUN → *DET. + PRON. + livre → *PRON. + livre → POSS. + livre = mon livre* "my book". Such a sequence of imaginary intermediate steps (here marked with an asterisk) is not only unnecessary, but harmful, since it treats *mon livre* and *le livre* (*qui est*) *à moi* as identical in meaning and obscures the difference (especially of connotation) between them. That certain of these intermediate combinations or constructions similar to them may have existed at an earlier time (e.g. DET. + POSS. + NOUN in Old French, as in *le mien livre*, lit. "the my book") is irrelevant. The introduction of such historical considerations would only serve to obscure the difference between Old and Modern French: the earlier stage of the language had *le mien livre* as a really existing construction, whereas the modern stage has lost it, and to pretend that it or something resembling it still exists, even in a hypothetical intermediate stage of transformation, is simply to falsify the facts of Modern French. Such intermediate steps and rules to generate them are useful only to instruct a machine—or a human whom one is treating as if he or she were a machine—to take a given in-put and produce a given out-put in wholly automatic fashion. For live speakers of real languages, our formulations must state the actual options open to them when they speak, and make clear the differences in meaning involved in the choice.

The entire procedure of formulating linguistic structures in terms of rules and exceptions has grown out of the description of dead languages, which could be treated as closed systems: Latin, Greek, Classical Hebrew, and certain modern literary languages (especially French and Italian) which have been artificially restricted in the same fashion. In such instances, there is a clear, permanently valid norm which can be treated as iron-clad, since for the dead languages there are no longer any native speakers using them for the basic purpose of language, namely every-day communication, and for the academically restricted forms of (say) French, the native speaker and his use of the language does not count. In foreign-language-learning, at the out-set it is valid to treat the target-language as if it were a closed system: the users of any language do have a certain core of phonological, morphological, syntactical and lexical features which the learner has to master in its entirety. But, at a more advanced stage, when the learner has completely mastered the new sets of habits inherent in the target-language, he has to learn what are the fluctuations, the alternations in their use that prevail among its speakers in their every-day living, so that he too can make the same choices that they do and convey or respond to the same differences in meaning.

Aside from their use in learning and using a classical, dead language, and in the elementary stages of learning a living language, rules have no place in linguistic description. They are a pedagogical device, and nothing more. Of course, any statement can be re-formulated as an instruction: instead of saying, for instance, "European men take off their hats to each other", we can say "If you want to do as European men do, take off your hat to other men". Such a re-formulation, involving a mere re-placement of a statement by a command (a transformation of the verb from indicative to imperative), is trivial; but there are two objections to the use of commands (rules) instead of statements in descriptive procedures. One is that description, in terms of functional units of structure, has to precede and underlie injunctions: you cannot command a person to do anything until you have a clear picture of what he is to do. (For a city, a complete guide-book cannot be constructed until the city is thoroughly mapped, in terms of streets, squares, blocks, and other functional units.) The other, even more important, is that no set of rules, however complete, is sufficient to describe (and hence to enable any machine or person to produce) the utterances possible in any living language. People simply do not talk according to rules, and (as we have seen) it is not enough to set up an ensemble of rules representing the "deep structure" of a language and its conversion into "surface structure", and then to assume that any departure therefrom on the part of a native speaker must be due to some exteriorly caused break-down in the generation of perfect sentences from a perfect "deep structure". A much better frame-work for the description of living humans' linguistic behavior is what might be termed the tagmemic-odic, which indicates the various possibilities of proceeding, once a speaker has embarked on a given construction, in a kind of flow-chart:

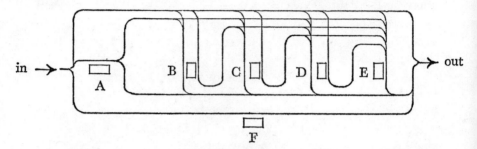

The lines on such a chart (of which the above is a very simple example) are analogous to paths, rather than to rail-way-tracks, because speakers on occasion jump unexpectedly from one path to another, with no reference to any "rule", either overt or implicit.

By the very nature of representation on paper, such a diagram is two-dimensional, and therefore best adapted to languages which have a primarily linear order of their elements in the flow of time. For languages such as Latin or Greek, with a freer syntactic order than (say) English or French, and with much more complicated morphological linkages between the component elements of constructions, a multi-dimensional representation of some kind would be more suitable. Certainly the transformational-generative approach, which is wholly linear, is totally unsuited to the "generation" of Latin or Greek utterances; sets of transformational rules, when prepared for even the simplest Latin phrase, prove to be both terribly complicated and highly unrealistic.

With respect to the element of time, there have been three approaches used, to date, in the presentation of language-structure: those customarily termed "paradigmatic" (which we might perhaps call "items-in-a-list"), "items-and-arrangement", and "items-and-process". In the first, a set of forms is simply listed, according to some structural characteristic (e.g. inflection for

case and number with nouns, or person and number with verbs),
and is often displayed in a two-dimensional diagrammatic arrangement, as in our school-grammars of Latin, Greek or other
highly inflected languages:

amō "I love"	amāmus "we love"
amās "thou lovest"	amātis "you love"
amat "he, she, it loves"	amant "they love"

In the second, a group of forms or equivalent syntactic combinations is enumerated and the order in which they are found is indicated, with no suggestion that anything has "happened" to
them aside from their collocation together. Thus, the Italian
phrase-type represented by *depòsito bagagli* "luggage-deposit",
campo pròfughi "refugee-camp", *scalo merci* "goods-station" can
be summarized as consisting of NOUN (HEAD) + NOUN (AT-
TRIBUTE), the latter not agreeing with the former in gender or
number, and indicating, in this instance, the beneficiary of the
referent of the former ("deposit for luggage", "camp for refugees",
"station for goods"). The "item-and-process" approach involves
treating any given form or construction as the result of a process
carried out on one or more others: e.g. Eng. *ate* ← PAST TENSE +
eat; It. *si* reflexive + *si* "impersonal agent" → *ci si,* as in *si diverte*
"he amuses himself" + *si* "impersonal agent" → *ci si diverte* "one
amuses oneself". Transformational-generative grammar is simply
an extension of the item-and-process approach to all items of
linguistic structure, whether it is appropriate to them or not, and
with an insistence on setting up intermediate steps in which only
one item is changed at a time, whether the intermediate steps thus
assumed exist or not: e.g., in the Italian phrase cited above, *si
diverte* + *si* → **si si diverte* → *ci si diverte.*

There has been considerable debate over the validity of these
various approaches, each with its partisans who have maintained
its exclusive claim to soundness. Actually, no one of the three is
exclusively valid: for certain types of material, one may be more
useful, and for other types, another. Where there are large sets

of forms differing from each other only in certain specific respects (e.g. categories of inflection), they may on occasion be most profitably listed in paradigmatic sets, which make their similarities and differences more evident to immediate inspection than do other types of presentation. In other instances, a construction may be irreducible to any more "basic" construction. The Italian NOUN + NOUN phrase discussed above had its historical origin in the ellipsis of a preposition introducing the second noun, e.g. *depòsito (per) bagagli* "deposit (for) luggage", etc. But at present, in many such combinations it is not possible to tell which preposition has been "left out" (does *vasto assortimento uòmini e bambini* come from *v. a. per u. e b.* "extensive assortment FOR men and children" or from *v.a. di u. e b.* "extensive assortment OF men and children"?). In some constructions of this type, the particular phrase came into use without there ever having been a preposition in the construction (e.g. *campo pròfughi* "refugee-camp"). Hence this Italian NOUN + NOUN phrase is now a separate construction in its own right, not involving any kind of ellipsis or deletion. In still other instances, an item-and-process or transformational formulation is much the most useful, as with It. *ci si* (above), or (say) Spanish *¡Lo cansada que estoy!* "How tired I [f.] am!" (with adjective variable for number and gender, but modifying invariable *lo*) ← *estoy cansada* "I [f.] am tired" + *lo estoy* "I am it (i.e. tired)".

Each of these approaches has its disadvantages, too. The first two may seem completely static, the first involving a bare listing and perhaps some visual arrangement, and the second simply an indication of linear (temporal) sequence. The third appears to be more dynamic than the first two, since it involves the carrying-out of a process; but the process is only fictional, and the resultant dynamicity likewise. As we have seen, all work on the synchronic axis of linguistic description necessarily involves the fiction that we can eliminate from our investigation all irreversible changes in linguistic structure, and to describe this latter as if no time were passing. There are two types of time involved: that which passes while the language is being used by its speakers, and that which passes while the observer is passing from one feature to another in his examination and description of the language. All synchronic approaches share the fiction that the first kind of time-factor can be eliminated. That the second kind is at all times to be eliminated as well, is the fiction underlying both paradigmatic and item-plus-arrangement presentation. When applied rigorously, they produce a completely static description, often requiring a more complicated and tortuous formulation than would the simple statement of a "process".

The "item-and-process" model involves a different fiction concerning the passage of time for the observer: that the passage of time MUST be taken into account, and hence the difference between one item and another MUST be described as if a change had taken place from one to the next (that is, as if the observer could never take in more than one item at a time). In the statement of any given "process", this fiction covers only the relation between the particular items involved; most descriptive grammars that are not of the rigorously item-and-arrangement type make more or less extensive, but still relatively unsystematic, use of grammatical "processes" in their formulations. Transformational grammar extends the fiction of a necessary passage of time for the observer to the entire description, and makes it basic to its presentation. Yet this assumption, too, is unrealistic; for both speaker and observer, choices, and options between them, do exist and are perceptible at the same time. More realistic than any of these three approaches, and hence in some ways to be preferred, is the "tagmemic-odic" approach discussed above (p. 78), which takes into account the necessary passage of time for the speaker while he is talking and also for the analyst while he is observing and formulating, but also recognizes the co-existence of choices and options, while still preserving the fiction of timelessness for the system as a whole for purposes of synchronic description.

Another danger inherent in treating a language as if it were a closed system capable (if not interfered with from outside) of producing only "well-formed sentences", is the temptation to concentrate on the utterance after it has been produced, and to correlate its structure only with that of other "well-formed sentences" and of a presumed "deep structure". This procedure concentrates attention unduly on the production of utterances by the speaker, and neglects the other, equally important half, of the speech-situation, namely the hearer. Any complete analysis of linguistic structure must take into account, not only the generation of audible speech by the talker, but its reception and interpretation by the hearer—and hence both the features which the former uses to convey meaning and those which signal it to the latter. This is why no approach through "well-formed sentences" can ever tell the whole story about language: people simply do not talk in "well-formed sentences" alone, nor yet in "well-formed sentences" and fragments thereof. (Consider the following complete and wholly meaningful dialogue: *Oh?—Yes, oh.*)

It is also why a linguistic description must enable the analyst or reader to move "upwards" or "downwards" from one level of structure to another (as in the diagram on p. 54). In actual speech-behavior, all levels of linguistic structure exist at the same time and interact with each other in all directions. For convenience in description, we may imagine the speaker as starting from the meanings he intends to convey and moving downwards to their "realization" in speech-sounds; but the listener has to proceed in the opposite direction so as to interpret what he hears. We may devise descriptions in which the phonemic level, for instance, is by-passed going "downwards", by setting abstract morphophonemic units and describing their "actualizations" in sound; but for the listener, the phonemic structure of what he hears is essential in order for him to interpret it. Take the speaker of Italian, who sees a moving-picture-advertisement showing a group of young men around a lady, with a caption OCCUPATI D'AMELIA. He has no way of knowing whether this stands for /okkupáti/ "occupied (m.pl.)" or /ókkupati/ "occupy thyself!

[82]

(2.sg. imperative)", until he hears it pronounced; when he does hear it, the signal which tells him how to interpret the form is the presence or absence of stress in the first syllable—a clear clue that stress is phonemic in Italian.[1]

Of these various frame-works, there is probably no single "best" one. Some may be more suitable for certain languages than for others. A transformational approach is certainly better adapted to English than it is, say, to Latin, and it is doubtful that it would be at all suitable for a "polysynthetic" American Indian language. The same may be true of various parts of the structure of one particular language: some types of phrases may best be treated by transformational formulation, others by item-and-arrangement formulation. An eclectic attitude, using more than one approach, is clearly the best to take towards the entire question of which frame-work to adopt. No matter which approach we adopt, however, our basic task remains the same: to identify, analyze, and formulate the relationships between recurrent partial similarities in as many utterances in the language as we can observe. At the out-set, while recording and beginning to analyze data, we must inevitably deal with all aspects of the language at once; in the end, regardless of which or how many different descriptive frame-works we work with, we must still perform the basic task of presenting the significant units of the language on all levels, and of stating their formal and semantic relationships to each other.

It is important, in presenting one's findings, to keep relationships of dependency and bondage clear. Language does not consist merely of words and their collocations. In most constructions, certain elements depend, as we have seen, on others; this relation-

---

1. Of course, if the reader knows that the movie is a version of Georges Feydeau's farce *Occupe-toi d'Amélie,* he has been tipped off in advance. But the naïve native speaker has no way of knowing this; and information from a foreign linguistic structure is never admissible in analyzing or formulating that of any language (e.g. Latin structure for English, that of French for Italian or Haitian Creole, etc.).

ship determines the classification and function of the elements involved. Failure to observe dependency-relationships may result in faulty analysis, as when two sequences like *money crisis* and *world crisis* are taken to be of the same type because each of them consists of two nouns written (in conventional spelling) separately. In actual pronunciation, they are quite different in structure and meaning: /mə́nij + kràjsis/ is a compound, with one full and one intermediate stress, and the first element indicates the object involved by the referent of the second ("crisis with respect to money"). The second, /wɔ́rld krájsis/, on the other hand, is a phrase containing two fully stressed nouns, with the first element indicating the extent of the second ("crisis extending over the world").

Bondage, similarly, is of major importance (as we saw on pp. 59–60) in determining the relationships of linguistic elements. Wherever relationships of bondage occur, they should never be neglected in either analysis or description. This is especially true of pidgin and creole languages, where apparent identity of forms with those of other languages (European or non-European) may impede the analyst from recognizing their true function unless he investigates their bondage-relationships. If, in dealing with Melanesian Pidgin, for instance, we start from a written representation based on English spelling, which separates words as in English, we will arrive at a bad misinterpretation of, say, such sentences as those which would be written as *you fellow make 'im all same me* "you [pl.] do like me" or *me look 'im one fellow balus 'e come* "I see an aeroplane coming", we will be tempted to think that *fellow, 'im, 'e* are all separate words, and will fail to realize that /-fɛlə/ is two suffixes (one added to pronouns indicating plural, and one added to adjectives); that /Im/ is an objective or transitive verb-suffix; and that /i-/ is a bound marker prefixed to third-person predicates.[2]

2. That these elements are, historically speaking, derived from the English noun spelled *fellow* and from the English pronouns spelled *him* and *he* respectively, is of course quite beside the point in this discussion.

Recognition of the status of these bound forms is essential for further analysis of Melanesian Pidgin structure in its own terms, not in those of either English or Melanesian languages.

The description of any linguistic structure must, in short, be as complete as possible, neglecting no aspect or level in favor of others, and likewise over-emphasizing no one part at the expense of others. It must be in terms of meaningful units, whose existence must be continually recognized even when statements of relationships go beyond them. The violent pendulum-swings of recent decades—away from the consideration of meaning, and back again to an over-emphasis on meaning; away from phonology, back to it; etc.—must be damped, and a scientific attitude restored. Above all, a mutual convertibility of frame-works must again be established, so that it will be possible to take all the discoveries of worth-while information about English and other languages that have been made and formulated in transformational-generative terms and to re-phrase them in a more widely acceptable and usable shape.

6

LANGUAGE CHANGES—BUT HOW?

Ever since Ferdinand de Saussure introduced into modern linguistics his unfortunate dichotomy between the absolutely synchronic and diachronic points of view (cf. p. 15), linguists have exercised a great deal of ingenuity trying to reconcile the two. The difficulties that they have experienced in so doing have been due, as we have seen, very largely to the unrecognized fictional nature of the *axe des simultanéités* or synchronic axis. The diachronic axis, on the other hand, is not at all fictional: time is forever passing, while we make our observations and formulations; and change, even though it be infinitesimal, and almost impossible to observe at any specific moment, is nevertheless always going on. Yet we are not justified, on this account, in rejecting the descriptive approach entirely and declaring, as did Hermann Paul, Berthold Delbrück and some more recent scholars, that language can be studied only from a historical point of view. The fiction of a synchronic view-point is highly useful in giving us a clearer picture than we would have if we did not adopt it. The question is, rather, how can we take both the "as if" static and the actually existing dynamic views of language into account? Where, in particular, is the bridge between the synchronic and diachronic points of view?

The bridge is to be found in the fact (p. 20) that no idiolect—and therefore, *a fortiori*, no dialect or language—is ever perfect

[87]

or in complete equilibrium. At any given point of time, there are always loosenesses in every individual's usage, many (though not necessarily all) of which he shares with other speakers in the community. Such loosenesses occur on all levels of linguistic structure. Many speakers of American English have at preent both the stop and the flap variants of intervocalic /t/ in words like *bitter, university;* both *dived* and *dove* as the past of *dive;* may say either *he has just come* or *he just came;* or may use both *inflammable* and *flammable* to refer to something that easily catches on fire. There are of course differences in connotation between the two members of each of these contrasting pairs, which serve, for each individual speaker, to keep them more or less apart. Often the connotation is one of free-and-easy vs. pedantic speech ([r] vs. [t] as variants of /t/); frequently it is one of old-fashioned vs. new (*dived* vs. *dove*). It may also involve differences in the meaning of a construction (*he has come, he came*); or it may reflect a possible confusion on one or both sides of an equivalence (does *inflammable* mean "very likely to catch fire" or "not likely to catch fire"?). These differences in connotation, meaning, or social standing furnish the fuel for the debates over such moot points, which constitute the permanent battle-ground of our purists, e.g. whether it is or is not "correct" to use *hike* in the sense of "raise, rise".

For each speaker and for the community as a whole, there is always, at any given time, a fluctuation in the frequency of these alternative forms, as between different speakers or different groups. A sufficiently detailed study could give us the number of times per day that several different speakers would use one allophone of /t/ rather than the other, and similarly for the frequency of *dived* vs. *dove* or any other competing pair. I do not know of any such studies having been made on any one idiolect or group of idiolects, by detailed examination of the usage of individual speakers—possibly because linguists have regarded idiolectal fluctuations as beneath their notice, through a misapplication of the old proverb *de minimis non curat lex*—but it would be very desirable for them to be made, on an idiolectal level. Some linguists have indeed made scattered and limited studies of such fluctuations in written documentations of current usage, e.g. the alternations in the agreement of past participles in Italian perfect phrases conjugated with *avere* "to have", in such alternations as that between *la tragedia che ho letta* "the tragedy which I have read" vs. *la tragedia che ho letto.* To be most informative, however, such studies should be carried out on large corpora of both spoken and written material, on all levels of formality and even including unpublished documents such as personal letters. A really extensive study of fluctuation in usage would probably have to be computerized in order to give serviceable results in a short enough time from its inception.

As time passes, the relative frequency of use, as between the competing items in any fluctuating usage, is likely to change. At first, behavior-pattern A is unchallenged: the usage of the community is undivided on that particular point. Pattern B arises, in the speech of one or more individuals, and, just because it seems to be an individual and hence non-significant peculiarity, goes virtually unnoticed. Then it is imitated by other speakers, to the point where it is a serious competitor of A. In the course of its extension, it is likely to acquire one connotation or another, depending on its origin and the channels through which it has spread. Its connotation may change, if the circumstances in which it is used change. For instance, the French sound-changes of /l̬/ to /j/, as in *famille* "family", and of /we/ to /wa/, as in *roi* "king", seem to have arisen in the seventeenth and to have spread in the eighteenth century, among the lower classes, and then to have risen to socially prestigious status at the time of the French Revolution, with the disappearance of the old aristocracy and the rise to prestige of formerly plebeian speakers.

It must not be thought, however, that the spread of innovations always takes place in one specific direction, socially or even geographically speaking, or at the same rate. When there is a firmly established ruling class and a more or less permanently in-

[89]

ferior proletariat or slave-population, such changes as spread will do so at a fairly slow rate, and from the upper class to the lower, as in traditional Spanish and Spanish-American society. If a hitherto less privileged class begins to rise socially (as in seventeenth-century France and eighteenth-century England), it will imitate its "betters" and the innovations will spread more rapidly, but still primarily "downward". "Upward" movement of linguistic or other patterns of behavior takes place primarily in periods of social upheaval (the Hundred Years' War and the Revolution in France, the Nazi period in Germany). Innovations normally spread from major centers of cultural prestige outwards to minor centers, and from these to even more out-lying regions, as the findings of linguistic geography show. But here, too, rustic patterns may enjoy a certain favor among the dominating groups, and countrified expressions may be borrowed into standard speech (e.g. "Down East" *boughten,* as an adjective, opposed to "home-made").

Nor do innovations, once they have begun to spread, always continue on an uninterrupted course of expansion until they have overcome their rivals, first pushing the latter into infrequent use or out-lying regions, and then replacing them entirely. On occasion, for one reason or another, an innovation may gain ground and then be checked or reversed in its spread. In fifteenth-century French, some speakers manifested a phonological development called "sigmatism", in which /r/ > /z/, so that *Paris* > /pazi/, *mon mari* "my husband" > /monmazi/, and so forth, including *chaire* "chair, pulpit" > /šezə/ and *béricle* "beryl, eyeglass" > /beziklə/. Through a strong reaction on the part of conservative speakers, pressure was brought against the use of /z/ and for the use of /r/ in these forms, and the alternants with /z/ went out of fashion. The only forms in which sigmatism survived were the relic words *chaise* "chair" (as distinguished from *chaire* "pulpit") and *bésicle* "eye-glass".

In other instances, an innovation and a conservative usage may survive side by side and continue in competition for a very long time, even centuries, without the conflict being resolved, and leaving manifold traces of divergent development in later stages of the language concerned. There seems to have been a long-lasting alternation in Latin between [au] and [ɔ:] (probably long and open), the former being the elegant pronunciation and the latter a vulgarism. At an earlier stage, when vowel length was significant in Latin, the [ɔ:]-alternant was interpreted by [au]-speakers as equivalent to their /o:/. Some vulgarisms were taken into non-vulgar speech with this equivalence, and are continued in the Romance languages with forms going back to PRom. /oˆ/ (= Lat. /o:/): e.g. Fr. *queue*, It. *coda* "tail" < PRom. /koˆda/ = Lat. /ko:da/ replacing *cauda* /kauda/. Later, when vowel-quality had replaced length as a distinctive feature of contrast in Popular Latin, the vulgar pronunciation with [ɔ:] was equated with open (lax) /o/, as shown by the continuation of PRom. /au/ with /o/ in such forms as It., Sp. *oro*, Fr. *or* "gold" < PRom. /auru/ = Lat. *aurum*.

Since linguistic systems are, first and foremost, sets of habits, whose systematic aspects can be analyzed into their constituent units,[1] it follows that linguistic change is to be viewed as alteration of these habits and of the units under which they are subsumed. These alterations can take place on the etic level, without affecting the pattern of contrast between significant units, and on the emic level. Needless to say, change takes place in all facets of linguistic structure, from phonology through lexicon. It may involve simple replacement of one feature by another, or split of one feature into two, or coalescence of two into one. The disappearance of a feature (e.g. the loss of Latin final -*s* and -*t* in Italian and Roumanian) might perhaps be considered a fourth type of change, but it is easier, from a purely book-keeping point of view, to regard it as "substitution by zero", so that it can be merged with the category of replacement.

1. We are using the term *constituent* here in its broad sense of "that which constitutes . . .", not in the narrow sense of *immediate* constituent in syntactic analysis.

Simple replacement on the etic level is well exemplified by the development of voiceless fricatives as positional variants of single (not double!) voiceless stops in intervocalic position, in Tuscan (cf. Table I). Although this replacement has existed for

PHONEME	ALLOPHONES	EXAMPLES
/p/	[ɸ] single, between vowels [p] elsewhere	}/pé^pe/ [ˈpeˆː-ɸe] "pepper"
/t/	[θ] single, between vowels [t] elsewhere	/dáto/ [ˈdaː-θo] "given" /tánto/ [ˈtanⁿ-to] "so much"
/k/	[x], [h] single, between vowels [k] elsewhere	/báko/ [ˈbaː-xo], [ˈbaː-ho] "silk-worm" /kíkko/ [ˈkik-ko] "seed"

TABLE I: *Tuscan Voiceless Stops and Fricative Allophones*

at least four or five centuries in Tuscan pronunciation, the fricatives have always remained positional variants of the stops, and so the variation is still on the phonetic level. Phonemic replacement may involve simply the position of a given phonological feature in the pattern of contrast, with no change in the sound-type involved, as in the development of Proto-Romance tense vowels out of Latin long vowels (cf. Table II), where the feature distinguishing the pairs of high-front, mid-front, high-back, and mid-back vowels from each other ceased to be that of length and was replaced by that of tenseness in four out of the five, disappearing altogether in the low vowel /a/. Both the sound itself and the relation of the phonemic unit to the rest of the pattern can change, as in the development of Proto-Romance /uˆ/ to French /y/, e.g. in /múˆru/ "wall" > /myr/ and many other forms.

On the morphological plane, when the English third-person singular ending -(e)*th* was replaced by -*s* (*singeth* ≠ *sings*, *saith* ≠ *says*), one allomorph was substituted for another. Replacement of morphemic units often takes the form of loss, as when the case-

[92]

LATIN		PROTO-ROMANCE	
/iː/ [i$^{(ˆ)}$ː]	/uː/ [u$^{(ˆ)}$ː]	/iˆ/ [iˆ(ː)]	/uˆ/ [uˆ(ː)]
/i/ [i$^{(ˇ)}$]	/u/ [u$^{(ˇ)}$]	/i/ [iˇ]	/u/ [uˇ]
/eː/ [e$^{(ˆ)}$ː]	/oː/ [o$^{(ê)}$ː]	/eˆ/ [e¨(ː)]	/oˆ/ [oˆ(ː)]
/e/ [e$^{(ˇ)}$]	/o/ [o$^{(ˇ)}$]	/e/ [eˇ]	/o/ [oˇ]
	/aː/ [aː]		/a/ [a]
	/a/ [a]		

MODERN FRENCH

/i/	/y/	/u/
/eˆ/	/œˆ/	/oˆ/
/e/	/œ/	/o/
/a/		/a>/
	/ə/	

TABLE II: *Vowel Systems of Latin Proto-Romance and Modern French*

system of Latin and Proto-Romance, involving a number of distinctive endings, was lost over the centuries in the nouns of all the Romance languages except Roumanian. Replacement of one morpheme by another is less frequent, but has occurred in the "pronouns of courtesy" in such Romance languages as Spanish and Italian. In the former, the noun-phrase *Vuestra Merced* "Your Mercy", common in the fifteenth and sixteenth centuries, has been replaced by *usted,* which is probably a borrowing from Maghrebian Arabic *ustād* "master", but influenced by *Vuestra Merced.* Individual forms may shift from one class of morphemes to another, as when the Old French nominative singular *on* "man" was "left out in the cold" by the disappearance of case as a category of inflection in the Middle French period, and shifted its allegiance, as it were, to the pronouns, becoming the Modern French indefinite *on* to refer to an unspecified actor.

In syntax, one variant feature of arrangement may replace another without changing the syntactic unit. Thus, in the mediaeval Romance languages, the past participle in a perfect phrase conjugated with descendants of PRom. /abé^re/ "to have" usually agreed with the direct object, no matter what the position of the latter (e.g. Old French *m'aṭ plevide sa feiṭ* "he has pledged me his faith", *Chanson de Roland,* v. 307). In seventeenth century French, mainly under puristic pressure, the past participle came to agree with a preceding direct object, but not with a following one: *il a regardé sa montre* "he looked at his watch", but *il l'a regardée* "he looked at it [i.e. the watch]". On the emic level, one syntactic unit may be substituted for another, as when the Latin nominal indirect-object complement (in the dative case), e.g. *patrī gladium dat* "he gives the sword to his father", was replaced in all the Romance languages except Roumanian by a phrase introduced by a preposition, as in French *il donne l'épée à son père,* Italian *dà la spada a suo padre.*

Lexical replacement is of two kinds, either substitution of one word for another in the same meaning, or development of a new meaning taking the place of an old one for the same word. Examples of both kinds of development are numerous and well known (indeed, perhaps the best known aspect of linguistic change, and the only one so far as the layman is concerned). Well-worn instances of the former are the replacement of Latin *magnus* "great" by French *grand,* It., Sp., Port. *grande;* Latin *multus* "much, many" by French *beaucoup* (de), It. *molto,* Sp. *mucho,* Port. *muito;* or Lat. *gladius* "sword" by the descendants of PRom. /spáta/ (Fr. *épée,* It. *spada,* Sp., Port. *espada*). The replacement of the sememes correlated with a given morpheme can be documented both for grammatical forms (e.g. the passage of German *sie* "they, them" to the meaning of "you", with the resultant wide-spread use of *die* for "they, them") and for words, in all kinds of changes of meaning, e.g. Lat. *testa* "potsherd > head", or *caballus* "nag > horse". A great deal of time and energy has been expended on classifying the replacements of sememes, e.g. "ennoblement" (OEng. *cwene* "woman" > Mod. Eng. *queen*), "degradation" (some Germanic cognate of Lat. *carus* "dear" > Eng. *whore*), and so forth, primarily in accordance with the social status accorded the words involved, at the times being compared.

Any linguistic unit can split in two, again on either the etic or the emic level. An allophonic, allomorphic, or allotaxic variation has to come about through the rise of non-significant alternants, as when pre-Tuscan [p t k] were replaced by [φ θ x] between vowels (cf. p. 92). Allomorphic split is exemplified in the rise of the non-significant variants of verb-roots in Romance, e.g. French /saš-/ *sach-* "know" beside /sav-/ *sav-*, or Spanish /kep-/ *quep-* "fit in" to /kab-/ *cab-;* allotaxic split, in the development of two word-orders for the Proto-Romance combination of PRE-DEFINITE-ARTICLE + NOUN, e.g. /illi ómo/ "the man" (> Fr. *l'homme* etc.) ~ /ómo illu/ (> Roumanian *omul*). Allosemic split develops whenever a word is used over a wider range of meaning than formerly, but remains the same morpheme, as when Lat. *servus* "slave" received in early mediaeval times the semantic extension "un-free farm-worker, serf". Allosemic variations are not normally indicated in spelling; one of the rare exceptions to this principle seems to have been the late literary critic Bernard DeVoto's graphemic distinction between the two allosemes of Eng. /fǽntəzi/, spelling it *fantasy* for the term as used in literary criticism, and *phantasy* when it is used in psychoanalysis.

Emic splits are well known on all levels of structure. The Proto-Romance phonemes /k/ and /g/ split, in Proto-Central-Western Romance, into /č/ and /k/, /ǧ/ and /g/, respectively: PRom. /kéˆra/ "wax" > PCWRom. /čéˆra/ (> It. /čéˆra/, OFr. /cirə/), and /gélu/ "cold" > PCWRom. /ǧélu/ (> It. /ǧélo/), but /káru/ "dear" and /gállu/ "rooster" remained as such. The Old French morpheme meaning "man", nom.sg. /on/, obl.sg. /omə/, split into the indefinite pronoun /õⁿ/ and the noun /om/ *homme* "man" in Modern French. Out of the Latin noun-phrase DEMONSTRATIVE + NOUN (in either order: e.g. *ille homo* or *homo ille* "that man"), there developed in Romance two phrase-types, DEFINITE ARTICLE + NOUN (with the definite article coming from an unstressed demonstrative), and demonstrative + noun: e.g.

[95]

Lat. *ille* (*illi*) *homo* "that" man > Fr. *l'homme* "the man" and (with *cet* < *ecce istu*) *cet homme* "that man". On the lexical level, one of the most wide-spread types of split is the development of a proper name into a common noun, while the proper name still continues in use, for instance *Victoria* as a woman's name and *victoria* "a kind of horse-drawn carriage", or, in Brazilian Portuguese, *Gillette* /žiléti/ as the trade-name of a kind of razor, and *gillette* (*gilete*) /žiléti/ "safety-razor" in general.

For merger, we may cite, on the phonological level, that which has taken place in the usage of many speakers of modern English, between /tr/ and /č/, /dr/ and /ǧ/, as when some-one says /čéjn/ for both *train* and *chain,* or /ǧéjn/ for both *drain* and *Jane*. Morphological merger took place when the two Latin verbs *ire* and *vadere* "to go" lost their separate identity and became suppletive allomorphs of one verb in Romance, e.g. Spanish *ir* (with, say, *voy* "I go"). On the syntactic level, a merger took place when the two Old Spanish constructions /ǧelo/ *ge lo* "to-him it (indef. obj. + dir. obj.)" and /selo/ *se lo* "to-himself it" were replaced, in Modern Spanish, by the single construction /selo/ *se lo* in both meanings: e.g. OSp. /ǧelodá/ *ge lo da* "he gives it to him" and /selodá/ *se lo da* "he gives it to himself" > Mod. Sp. /selodá/ *se lo da* for both. Word-blending is widely known, especially in humorous formations, such as Lewis Carroll's famous "portmanteau-words" in his poem *Jabberwocky* (in *Through the Looking-Glass*), such as *chortle = chuckle × snort*.

Complete innovations, creations absolutely *ex nihilo,* are at the present stage of humanity's linguistic development virtually unknown so far as phonological elements are concerned. The range of sounds which humans can make is limited by the structure of their breathing-apparatus; I do not know of any instance where, in normal every-day usage, a completely new sound-type or phoneme has suddenly been introduced into material previously used by the speakers of a language. (It is said that, in Indonesia, the language-academy decreed the introduction of a previously unknown phoneme so as to enrich the combinatory possibilities of the language; but this was an artificial procedure, whose effect on real language-behavior might eventually filter down from learnèd to ordinary speakers, but only over a long period of time and undistinguishably from any other foreign influence.) New sound-types or phonemes come in, normally, through foreign borrowings, such as /báx/ *Bach* or /lēžəri/ *lingerie* in English, with the unfamiliar phonemes /x/ and /ē/ respectively. When such borrowings occur, they are often misheard by naïve speakers who have not mastered the pronunciation-habits involved, with resultant distortions like /bák/ and /langəré/ or the likes. In morphology and syntax, likewise, sudden innovations come about primarily as a result of foreign borrowings, such as the introduction of -*s* plurals into Mexican Indian languages through large-scale lexical borrowings from Spanish, or the English syntactic types *But certainly!* (imitated from French *Mais certainement!*) and *Operation Cross-Roads* (also imitated from French). Van Helmont's *gas,* Gelett Burgess's *blurb,* and George Eastman's *kodak* are the stock examples of words invented by specific individuals and having specific meanings from the out-set (but formed out of the existing phonological stock of the language involved and fitting into existing morphological and syntactical patterns). In the coinage of trade-names, extensive use has been and is being made of hitherto unutilized combinations of phonemes into syllables, e.g. *Fab, Dreft, Omo.* (For some reason, soaps and detergents seem to be the favorite recipients of such invented names.)

Not only single units of linguistic structure, but their patterning, undergoes change in the course of time. Table II (p. 93) shows three of the stages in the development of the Modern French vowel-system from that of Latin; many intermediate stages, as well, could and should be listed in a structural history of the language. Morphological sub-systems change through the loss of old form-classes or categories of inflection, and the rise of new ones. Thus, in English, the old Indo-European category of grammatical gender (not, in itself, related to either animation or

[97]

sex, but wholly a feature of morphological linkage in syntactic combinations) has been completely lost in both nouns and pronouns; it has been replaced by nothing in nouns and by sex-reference in pronouns.[2] In Brazilian Portuguese every-day speech, the second person has been wholly lost as a category of inflection, since *tu* "thou" and *vos* "ye" have been replaced by such forms as *você* "you" or *o senhor* "the gentleman" and *a senhora* "the lady" in direct address, all with third-person agreement. As a result, colloquial Brazilian Portuguese has only two persons in its verb-inflection, first and non-first. When one hears a non-first-person form like *vai* "goes", it is only from the context (linguistic or non-linguistic) that one can tell whether the form is addressed to oneself or to some other person. Whole sets of vocabulary-items, representing fields of meaning, die out or come into being in correlation with changes in the non-linguistic world, as witness the obsolescence of terminologies like those of falconry and armor, and the rise of new ones like those of electronics or human flight.

How about the more basic features of language-design? Are there changes in their relation to each other? Does duality of patterning undergo alteration, for instance, or does productivity as such ever cease? On the whole, our answer must be negative, at least as far as real-life language is concerned. Artificial languages like Esperanto or Ido are endowed by their inventors with the basic design-features of real-life languages, including both duality and productivity. (Non-languages like those of formal logic and computer "language" need not concern us.) Productivity is sharply limited whenever a language is "reduced to rule", as traditional grammarians put it, either through the natural process of losing all its native speakers (as happened with Classical Latin, Greek, Sanskrit, or Hebrew), or through authoritarian limitation,

---

2. As shown by the obligatory use of *he* to refer to male beings, *she* for females, and *it* where sex is either absent or irrelevant (e.g. for a baby). "Personification" and similar phenomena are instances of arbitrary ascription of sex; "depersonification" (e.g. referring to a disliked person as *it*) is arbitrary denial of sex.

[98]

as in the Académie Française ideal for French. Yet, even here, productivity does not disappear totally, since analogical formation of a regular kind, according to officially sanctioned rules, is still permitted. If productivity ceases entirely, a speaker becomes like a gramophone record, in that he can repeat what he has heard but is unable to make up new expressions of his own accord. This phenomenon has been observed in the case of the last speakers of "dying" American Indian languages, one of whom observed "It's not good you learn too many languages. It broke your language. You can't speak plain."

How about creativity, that catch-word of the idealistic and transformational-generative schools? Are speakers not continually creating new linguistic material and patterns? Here, the answer is decidedly no—not at the present stage of human language-development. There must have been a time, perhaps hundreds of millennia ago, when proto-humans were elaborating what eventually became human language, and when some "pre-languages" may have lacked all the major design-features that all languages now have. For such a stage, we can justifiably surmise that new basic features of design and new linguistic habits were being literally created, i.e. brought into existence where nothing existed before. That stage of human linguistic development, however, is long since past. All the languages attested or reconstructible, for as far back as we can extend our time-perspective, are of the same basic type, and nothing new has been added. Speakers are of course always producing novel utterances, ones which have never been heard before and will never be heard again; but these and all other utterances are always made of pre-existing linguistic material, on the basis of pre-existing patterns or analogical extensions thereof. Novelty is not the same as creativity; the latter has not for a long time been, is not, and will not be in any foreseeable future a characteristic of human language.

Innovations come into a linguistic system from two main sources: within the system itself, or outside of it. A feature may be present in some part of the system, but not in another; it can then be extended to a part where it has not previously been present. This process, which may be termed *internal* or *intrasystemic* borrowing, is customarily known as *analogy*. It may manifest itself on all levels of linguistic structure. In phonetics, it involves the transfer of allophones from their earlier environment to positions where their occurrence is no longer automatic: e.g. Puerto Rican Spanish [h] as a variant of /s/ at the end of a syllable (as in [loh'lapiseh] *los lápices* "the pencils") being extended to syllable-initial position (as in [lo'hotroh] *los otros* "the others"). Phonemic analogy, misapplied, leads to over-correction: a well-known example is that of the substitution of /mjúwn/ *mewn* for /múwn/ *moon,* by speakers who have been told to pronounce *tune* as /tjúwn/, not as /túwn/. Morphological analogy is perhaps the best-known of all, with transfers such as that of the *-o-* of the past tense from *drive drove* to *arrive arrove* (p. 49). In syntax, it is analogical substitution that leads to the extension of, say, *you and I* as a set group in constructions like *between you and I,* since speakers are told to use *you and I* instead of *you and me* in other environments ("say *you and I are going home,* not *you and me is going home*"). Semantic change is also a type of analogical extension, when a form acquires a new meaning through parallelism with other forms in the same environment, e.g. *presently* "soon > under present circumstances", parallel to *normally* "under normal circumstances" or *ordinarily* "under ordinary circumstances".

Borrowing from outside a given linguistic system, or *extrasystemic* borrowing, can take place under any circumstances, from any other system. Some scholars have distinguished types of borrowing according to the source from which they are made. In *dialectal* borrowing, the source is a mutually intelligible dialect of the same "language", as in Am. Eng. *be sot in one's ways,* or *crack hardy* "act as if one were bold"; Austr. Eng. *possum* "talk about a subject with many excursuses", or *gum-tree* "eucalyptus". Both *intimate* and *cultural* borrowings would involve the imitation of foreign languages, the former in situations of close interpersonal contact (e.g. Eng. *skirt* from Scandinavian during the period of symbiosis between Englishmen and Danes in the Middle Ages), and the latter in less close contact, often through impersonal media of communication such as written sources, and more recently radio, movies, and television. All intellectuals can be involved in either of these types of borrowings, with the homely predominating in intimate but not absent from cultural borrowing (cf. for the latter, such Italian culinary terms as *pizza*, *spaghetti*, and *lasagne* in American English). Examples of a more "high-falutin'" type of cultural borrowing are legion, such as *intelligentsia* from Russian, *joie de vivre* or *esprit de corps* from French, *Zeitgeist* or *Weltschmerz* from German, *et cetera ad infinitum* (from Latin).

Cutting across this classification by types of source is another classification of borrowings by the relation between form and meaning. A word simply taken from another language, with an approximation of both the phonological shape and the meaning it has in the source-language, is a loan-word, such as those cited in the previous paragraph. If, however, on the model of a given range of meaning in another language, the meaning of a word is extended, this semantic change is variously termed a *loan-shift*, a *loan-translation*, or a *calque*—for instance, Latin *cāsus* "a fall" being extended to mean "an inflected form of a noun", on the model of Greek πτῶσις, which meant both. On occasion, a form is borrowed and then partially re-shaped in accordance with some word in the borrowing language which seems to be similar in meaning and/or form; we then have a *loan-blend*, such as Melanesian Pidgin *blaistik* "pencil", from German *Bleistift* but with the second element re-made on the model of *stik* "stick".

Elements on all levels of structure can pass from one language to another by the process of borrowing. They do so normally, however, in free forms which are borrowed as units, bringing their constituent elements with them. It was through the flood of French loan-words, for instance, in the Middle English period, that we received such features as the phonemic

[101]

contrast between /f/ and /v/, which had previously been sub-phonemic; hosts of prefixes and suffixes like *en-, non-, pur-, -age, -ity, -ment;* and at least a strong impulse towards the generalization of the plurals in *-s* at the expense of those in *-er* and in *-en.* Such borrowings take place through bilingual speakers who have at least some knowledge (by no means always perfect) of the foreign language, from which they carry over the various kinds of loans into their own speech. They are then imitated by other speakers, whether the latter be mono- or bilingual. Even in the case of bookish loans, the ultimate origin is in the speakers of the source-language whose written notation of their speech has been read and re-interpreted by the speakers of the borrowing language.

There is one kind of situation, however, in which the original carry-over of habits from one language to another is not due to this kind of imitation. When a speaker of language A learns language B imperfectly, he carries over some of his habits into the new language. He may talk it with a "foreign accent"; bring in morphosyntactic habits through loan-translation, as do (for instance) Indian speakers of English when they say *He wants that I go* instead of *He wants me to go;* or introduce words from their first language into their new one, especially if the latter has no exact equivalent therefor, such as Yiddish *schnorrer* "socially accepted cadger" or *nudnik* "nuisance". If the descendants of such people go over to speaking language B exclusively, and have no other model to imitate than their parents' or grand-parents' imperfect reproduction of its patterns, their variety thereof will of course perpetuate the habits carried over from language A. If the inhabitants of a given region go over to speaking a new language brought in by another (usually a conquering) group, their earlier language is called a *substratum* (manifested, for example, in the continuation of the Oscan-Umbrian sound-change of *-nd-* to *-nn-* and *-mb-* to *-mm-* in the Latin of Pompeii and in modern Neapolitan). If, on the other hand, the members of a conquering group abandon their earlier language and speak only the language used in the region where they have settled, the earlier language is termed a *superstratum* (e.g. the languages of the Germanic invaders in the Romance-speaking territories, as manifested, say, in Visigothic stress-patterns continued in Old Spanish anisosyllabic verse). The influence of a substratum- or superstratum-language is to be explained, not as the result of inherited physical differences in the speech-organs (for which there is no valid evidence), nor of the atavistic survival of earlier speech-patterns in a (non-existent) "collective unconscious", nor of some mystical psychic miasma affecting any-one who comes to live in a given region, but only as the relic of a period of bilingualism, through the process of imperfect language-learning and transmission of its results, as described in this paragraph.

7

LANGUAGE CHANGES—BUT WHY?

Strictly speaking, the title of this chapter is an anachronism. For many generations, grammarians and linguists have been asking the question: "Why does language change?", and finding the answer in various factors which one scholar or another has thought should be emphasized—the influence of race, heredity, climate, and so forth. But their starting-point has normally been the assumption that language ought not to change; that, if no outside factors were at work, any given language, or indeed the institution of human language as a whole, would remain immutable. Such a notion was quite understandable in ancient or mediaeval times, when the only language to which any analytical attention was paid was one classical language or another (Latin, Greek, Hebrew), taught in the schools according to a set grammatical dogma expressed in rules. It was easy to regard the "grammatica" as unchanging, and any variation therefrom in popular speech as due merely to ignorant or lazy speakers' unwillingness to learn and obey the rules.

In the last two centuries and more, however, enough evidence has accumulated to show that human language is always changing, and that Dante was right when he wrote, as early as the 1290's, in the *De vulgari Eloquentia* (I.ix.6):

Since, therefore every human language [. . .] has been re-
made in accordance with our whims since the confusion of

[105]

the Tower of Babel [. . .] and since man is a most unstable and changeable being, language cannot be long-lasting nor stable; but like other human things, such as customs and dress, it has to vary in space and time.

As we have seen, no idiolect is ever absolutely stable and fixed in the ordinary behavior of any individual, since irregularities, fluctuations, and generally unpredictable behavior are always present. Every-one is always making slips, blends, corrections, and innovations through analogy or borrowing. This lack of fixity is bound to be reflected in the usage of every living speech-community. Under such circumstances, how could languages, and language as a human institution, fail to change?

Our problem, in connection with linguistic change, needs to be phrased, rather, in some such way as this: given the universality and inevitability of change in linguistic structure, with what can we correlate it? We may begin by dismissing various broad correlations that have been suggested, because there is no evidence to support them. One factor often mentioned is climate: for instance, it has been suggested that French developed nasal vowels because of the damp, foggy climate of Paris and the central Seine valley. However, as Kr. Nyrop pointed out, Portuguese also has nasal vowels, although it is spoken in a climate which is generally bright, sunny, and dry. Even the type of dwelling used by a speech-community has been suggested as a possible factor: some languages are said to have subtle distinctions (e.g. a wealth of laryngeal consonants, as in Arabic) because they are spoken mostly indoors, where fine shadings of sound can be perceived more easily than under the unfavorable acoustic conditions prevailing out-of-doors. But is Arabic not spoken in the desert also, where sound will not carry as easily as it does inside a house?—and do not the languages of the North-West Pacific coast Indians, who certainly spent plenty of time out-of-doors, have even more complicated systems of velars, gutturals, and laryngeals?

The influence of heredity, also, has been a favorite recourse of theorists. "Common sense" would seem to suggest that a difference in race would indicate a difference in the shape of the vocal organs or of the brain, and hence also in the ability of members of a given race to produce a given sound, to make a given morphological or syntactic combination, or to grasp a given meaning. Extensive experience and research has shown that no such correlation exists: all members of the human race have the same structure of the organs used in phonation, of the nervous system and of the brain, and, if brought up in a given speech-community, will learn to speak the language of that community in exactly the same way as any other of its members. A more recent and slightly more sophisticated version of the heredity-hypothesis has sought to correlate phonological features, and more specifically the presence or absence of the interdental fricatives [θ] and [$\eth$], with blood-types. Exactly through what mechanism the predominance of one blood-type or another in a population would influence the structure of the tongue and the teeth, their positioning to produce these sounds, or the structure of the brain in such a way as to affect the innervation of the messages sent to the organs of speech, was never made clear by the proponents of this correlation. In any case, the correlation was set up only as between the standard languages of national states (Portugal, Spain, France, etc.) and the blood-types statistically predominant in those countries, without taking into account the wide variation in regional dialects, so that it was based on quite insufficient data.

Such correlations as, to date, have seemed relatively valid have been established in quite different directions—with intrasystemic factors in the structure of languages themselves, and with extrasystemic factors of a social nature. In general, and from an over-all point of view, we can say that linguistic change takes place without reference to the intentions of the speakers themselves. Earlier generations—especially in the middle of the nineteenth century, when Darwinist imagery was wide-spread in discussions of scientific method—often referred to sound-change as taking place according to "iron laws", acting wholly apart from the will or even the awareness of individual speakers, similarly to the "laws" of physics or of the heredity of organisms. This formulation of the nature of linguistic change is certainly not tenable, if taken literally: the behavior of humans when speaking is in no wise comparable to that of inanimate objects in motion, nor yet are languages living organisms.

Yet it remains true that individual volition or teleology has little or no effect on the over-all development of a language over the decades or centuries, and still less on that of human language as a whole through the millennia. Each of us may, at times, have some little personal goal that he hopes to achieve with regard to his own usage: I remember, for instance, having had, as a high-school student, the specific aim of making my speech such that no-one could tell from what part of the English-speaking world I came. Even that was, of course, a hopeless aim; the most that any individual can hope to achieve is certain stylistic effects (clarity, effectiveness, impressiveness of one sort or another) by exercising a skillful choice among the options available to him in his idiolect which he has learned that his community will accept. As for influencing others, it takes a dictatorial personality like that of François de Malherbe, in a particularly insecure community like that of early seventeenth-century France, to impose one's will for even a short time, with regard only to certain moot points. The effect of such dictatorial rule never spreads beyond a relatively small, select group, nor does it last in depth for more than a few decades. In the long run, the effects of Malherbe-type language-dictatorship are at best diffuse and survive only sporadically, in "gesunkenes Kulturgut" which becomes part of a community's folk-lore concerning language, such as the belief that "good style" forbids the repetition of any given word within a sentence, or that liaison, in French, is made for "euphony". As for the possibility of any one person's influencing the fundamental structure of a whole language, it has been wisely observed that not even Dante could have made Tuscan into a tone-language.

[108]

It follows, *a fortiori*, that any effort on the part of, say, philosophers or logicians to change the structure of a language in accordance with their desires to establish a thoroughly systematic, water-tight frame of discourse, would be hopeless from the outset. That they should attempt to construct systems of formal logic or other types of symbolism for their own ratiocinations is, of course, their privilege. But such restricted systems will always remain suitable only for narrow, specialized discourse, without the looseness and adaptability which are essential for the functioning of ordinary language in every-day life—and which are also at the root of inevitably uncontrollable change in language over the centuries. This consideration disposes, also, of the theory that changes in linguistic structure have come about as the result of some kind of collective change in philosophical out-look on the part of a speech-community as a whole. It has been suggested, for example, that the Latin future was lost, during the late Roman Empire, because, with the rise of Christianity, the speakers of Latin came to believe that there was no future for man-kind and that it was therefore unnecessary to talk about anything with future-tense verbs. That any such change in people's day-to-day out-look actually took place, is rather doubtful; if anything, the loss of the Latin future was the result, rather, of phonemic changes which resulted in troublesome homonymy between the future and other tenses. Changes in people's out-look do not cause them to intentionally change their language-structure. This latter is quite independent of communities' views on philosophy, religion, politics, etc.: the most convinced atheist and the most deeply religious man will use the same linguistic structure to debate in, or the most reactionary Czarist and the most radical Bolshevist.

One more wide-spread theory concerning linguistic change needs to be mentioned, that which would ascribe it to a presumably universal human trend towards making as little effort as possible. According to this theory, certain sounds would be inherently easier to produce, certain forms or syntactic combina-

[109]

tions easier to generate, than others, and there would be an over-all trend towards ease in speech. Yet there is so little actual effort involved in speaking, especially for some-one using his native idiolect, that the difference in effort required to pronounce, say, [ke] as compared with [če], or to make a noun and a modifying numeral agree in number (Eng. *three books*) as opposed to refraining from making such an agreement (Hung. *három könyv*, lit. "three book"; cf. p. 42), is minimal. Language has often been compared to a low-energy control-system, similar in some ways to a servo-mechanism which acts as a trigger to set off much larger expenditures of energy than are involved in its own operation (cf. p. 41).

This appeal to "least effort" is, in a way, related to earlier theories according to which languages had periods of growth, full ripeness, and decay. The modern period of any given language was always interpreted as involving decay, due to speakers' unwillingness to exert themselves and put in the necessary effort on using the language correctly (cf. p. 105). When it was first observed that the general trend of the modern Indo-European languages was towards simplification, it was interpreted as representing the same type of decay from the "perfection" of the proto-language. We have already seen (p. 40) the fallacy underlying this view, which is based on a faulty metaphor of a language as an organism. Equally fallacious is its inversion, suggested by Otto Jespersen, that the modern stages of the Indo-European languages represent, not decay, but progress. In fact, morphological simplification, as in English or Danish, is counterbalanced by a corresponding syntactical complication. Merit ("perfection", "decay") in language can be defined only in terms of non-linguistic criteria; even then, no language is intrinsically, permanently unadaptable to changed requirements in the cultural environment in which it is used.

Any single simplified theory of linguistic change is bound to be insufficient, because of the numerous and complicated interrelations between the different planes of structure, and because of the various influences affecting language coming from non-linguistic sources. What may seem, at any given time, to be a fairly minor and unimportant change in habits (especially of pronunciation, which normally goes on almost wholly outside of speakers' awareness) can bring about far-reaching changes in other parts of the structure. The classical example of this type of chain-reaction is the Middle French conditioned sound-change of /s/ in syllable-final pre-consonantal position, first to [h] and then to length of the preceding vowel phoneme, as in /bestə/ ['bestə] "animal" > ['bɛhtə] > /beːtə/ ['bɛːtə]. The majority of nominative singular and oblique plural case-forms in nouns, and a great many person- and number-endings in verbs, however, ended in /-s/, and were inevitably affected by the conditioned change and later loss of final /-s/. After a lengthy period of extensive fluctuation and readjustment—lasting from the fourteenth century to the present, and not yet over—the entire French morphological and syntactical system has been re-shaped as a result. An extensive system of liaison-alternations (e.g. *vous allez* /vuzaleˆ/ "you go" vs. /vušāteˆ/ *vous chantez* "you sing") has developed. The spoken form of most nouns is the same in the singular and the plural: e.g. /ləša/ *le chat* "the cat", /leˆša/ *les chats* "the cats". The presence of a subject (noun or pronoun) together with the verbal predicate in a major clause has become obligatory: e.g. /zəšat/ *je chante* "I sing", /tyšāt/ *tu chantes* "thou singest", /ilšāt/ *il chante* "he sings", as opposed to Old French /čantə/ *chant*, /čantəs/ *chantes*, /čantəθ/ *chantet̬* for these three meanings.

In the extensive and subtle inter-play of changes like these on the various planes of linguistic structure, there are the two main factors which we discussed and exemplified in the previous chapter. Changes on the etic level do not, by definition, affect meaning, and are subject primarily to the whims of fashion, as Dante pointed out (pp. 105–106). Changes on the emic level involve, not the characteristics of the phenomena themselves, but the patterning of their relation to each other. If a purely phonetic replacement of one sound by another takes place, it makes no difference for the hearer, so far as the denotational meaning is concerned, although there may be differences in connotation, e.g. of regional dialect or social class, depending on the use of one variant or another. A shift in habit can thus take place, without comprehension being affected, and hence without much of any attention being paid to it. Thus, the use of intervocalic [ɸ θ x] in Italian (p. 92) signals to the hearer simply that the speaker is a Tuscan, since there is no contrast between [p] and [ɸ], etc., in either Italian or in Tuscan regional speech. But, once a shift in habit has taken place, simply because it involves a habit, it becomes fixed and no attention is paid to it.

However, when a further change on the etic level brings into contrast features which were previously not in contrast, the difference now becomes significant and hence, by definition, emic. Suppose, for instance, that a new intervocalic [p t k] were to arise in Tuscan—perhaps through simplification of intervocalic double consonants, with such a change as /bákko/ *Bacco* "Bacchus" > */báko/. Now ['bako] will mean one thing, such as "Bacchus", and ['baxo] another, in this case "silk-worm". So we will then have /báko/ and /báxo/ in contrast, and there will be two phonemes /k/ and /x/; and similarly for the pairs /t/ and /θ/, /p/ and /ɸ/. Such a change on the emic level always has to take place in two steps: the rise of an etic variant and a shift in habits from one variant to the other; and the coming of a second etic change which sets up a contrast where previously there had been only a non-significant variation. But, by the time the second change has taken place, it is too late to reverse the first, because confusion will result therefrom; so the new situation has to remain, and another emic change has come about. The situation has aptly been compared to the process of walking, with the weight of the body resting first on one foot and then on the other.

In a large, multidialectal community such as that of Latin in late Republican and in Imperial times, or those of the modern world languages, a further complication arises, that of cross-dialectal misunderstanding. Speakers of one dialect, with a given distribution of features, hear speakers of another, with the same or closely similar features differently distributed, and misinterpret the situation. In my own speech I have only [tᴜ] and [dᴜ] (alveolar stop followed by velarized retroflex semi-vowel) for /tr/ and /dr/. When I hear other speakers use [tř] and [dř] in the same function, these seem to me like my own [tš] and [dž]. Were I to imitate such speakers (say, for reasons of social prestige), I would do so with my [tš] and [dž], and would thereby be merging my earlier /tr/ and /dr/ with my /č/ and /ǧ/, and saying /čéjn/, /ǧéjn/ for *train* and *drain* (as, indeed, some speakers actually do; cf. p. 96). Misinterpretations of the same kind also take place on the morphological, syntactical, and lexical planes, leading to over-corrections and malapropisms—as when some-one substitutes a verb-form in the wrong place and comes out with *I have wented* instead of *I have gone,* or uses *hypothecate* in the meaning of hypothesize ("We must hypothecate three numbers and three genders for Proto-Indo-European").

There has been a long debate, by now nearly a century old, over the relation of phonological change to that on the morphological and syntactical plane. The principle that soung-change is regular was implicit in the work of linguists in the first part of the nineteenth century (Rask, Grimm, Bopp, Diez). It was made explicit by the *Junggrammatiker* (Brugmann, Leskien, Meyer-Lübke) in the 1870's and following decades, with the formulation that sound-change was absolutely regular and "permitted of no exceptions", proceeding by "iron laws" (cf. p. 108) and physical in nature, whereas the replacement of morphological and syntactic features was chiefly the result of analogy, conceived of as "psychological" (as opposed to physical) in its origin. We need not go into the long and discouraging history of the debates over the theoretical pronouncements of the *Junggrammatiker,* except to point out that there was a great deal of misunderstanding on both sides, but especially on that of their opponents (Curtius, Johannes Schmidt, Schuchardt). The term *Junggrammatiker* and

[113]

its English and Romance equivalents (*Neo-Grammarian*, etc.) have by now come to be little more than cuss-words, and had best be abandoned, except as a historical term to refer to Brugmann, Leskien, and their immediate followers. Yet the issue of sound-change and its regularity is central to our understanding of the factors underlying change in linguistic structure as a whole. We shall therefore endeavor to discuss, first the relation of phonological and morphosyntactic change to the basic design of human language, and then the reasons for assuming a fundamental regularity in sound-change.

It has long since been observed that phonological change proceeds in complete independence of morphology, syntax, and meaning. Of course, the effects of sound-change may be overlaid by developments on other levels of structure, in such well-known replacements as that of Old French /liévəθ/ *lievet* "he raises" (> PRom. /lévat/) by Modern French /lev/ *lève,* on the analogy of forms which developed without the diphthong in unstressed position, such as /ləvons/ *levons.* Such over-lay by no means constitutes an exception to the sound-change itself, only an interference with its results. It is possible for phonological change to be so independent because the sound-system of each language is on a separate level of patterning, as a result of the duality that we have already discussed (p. 55). Any phonological system, looked at synchronically, is a set of habits of making noises, which are quite independent of the grammatical or semantic patterns of the language involved. (Even onomatopoeia, as has often been remarked, is highly conventionalized and fits within the phonemic system of whatever language is being spoken.) Hence it is to be expected that, when people's habits of making noises change, they should change in and for themselves, as a separate part of the total linguistic system.

Morphological and syntactic habits change in a radically different fashion, by borrowing (as we have seen, pp. 99–103), from either within a system (i.e. by analogy) or outside of it. Internal borrowing is the direct manifestation of the other most important design-feature of linguistic structure, productivity. All human communication by means of language is made possible by the fact that we can produce novel utterances, on the analogy of others that we have either said ourselves or heard from others. But our systems themselves are not complete or in total equilibrium, and the analogies by which we produce novel formations (morphological, syntactic, lexical) are far from perfect. Inevitably, therefore, the possibilities for unusual formations, different from those that have gone before, are open-ended, so that competing forms or constructions can arise, fluctuate, and eventually either replace earlier ones or recede (cf. Chapter 6). External borrowing (from another dialect or language) is possible because of a third design-feature, namely receptivity. Humans are not limited, as most other living beings seem to be, in the number of meaningful combinations that they can make with the phonological material at their disposition in any one linguistic system. If there are gaps in the patterning of their forms, constructions, or meanings, those gaps can be filled through imitation of what speakers find in other sources than their own speech. This is why it is futile to condemn any language for supposed "inefficiency": as the sixteenth-century Italian G. B. Gelli put it:

> All languages are suitable to meet the needs of those who speak them; or, if they are not, their users make them so.

That the functional use (though not necessarily explicit formulation) of the criterion of regularity in sound-change was the key to the great forward strides made in historical and comparative linguistics in the nineteenth century, has by now been recognized by all competent historians of the field. There were anticipations of this principle well before the nineteenth century, especially in the work of the sixteenth-century Italian linguist and phonetician Claudio Tolomei, whose explicit statement (made *à propos* of the development of Latin *pl-* to Italian *pi̯-*) deserves to be cited every time the question of historical priority in the formulation of the principle arises:

[115]

. . . And I would be so bold as to say that in the original and pure speech of Tuscans, this [i.e. Lat. *pl-* > It. *pi̯-*] was a universally valid rule, and that all those words which are now written differently, such as *plora* "he weeps", *implora* "he implores," *splende* "it is resplendent", *plebe* "populace" and the like, were not taken from the middle of the town-squares of Tuscany [i.e. from every-day speech], but were set up by writers, and by some-one who wished to enrich the language, preferring to use them in the form in which he found them written in Latin, without giving them the form of Tuscan speech [i.e. without substituting *pi-* for *pl-*] . . . because without a doubt the common usage of earlier times would, had it inherited these words, have said *piora, impiora, spiende,* and *pieve,* and we have manifest evidence of this latter in that in the vernacular we call *pieve* a church devoted to the religious services of the common people.

This passage from Tolomei contains, not only in germ, but fully developed, all the essential features of historical linguistic methodology, so far as the development from one stage of a language to another is concerned: the recognition of regular phonemic change, of exceptions thereto, of their explanation by borrowing (in this case of learnèd origin), and of the resultant existence of doublets (*plebe* "populace" ~ *pieve* "church for the populace"). Unfortunately for the development of linguistics, interest in sober, fact-based historical study of this kind was replaced in the following century by aprioristic speculation on "universal grammar" of the Port-Royal type, and linguistics did not regain a solid scientific base until the latter part of the eighteenth century.

As Otto Jespersen remarked, it was a curious fact that, as a result of the extensive debates over the principle of "phonetic law" in the late nineteenth century, very few scholars accepted the doctrine in theory, but virtually all followed it in practice. This was, as is well known, because the principle itself was very badly stated by Leskien in his formulation "Phonetic laws admit of no exceptions" (Die Lautgesetze *kennen keine Ausnah-men*), and also because the opposition thereto—based as it was on Leskien's dogmatic statement and emotional reactions against it and the way it was presented—did not come to grips with the real issues. The term *law* was out of place in this discussion, since nothing nomothetic is involved, and the individual sound-changes customarily called "laws" (Grimm's, Verner's, Bartsch's, etc.) are single historical events, not general "laws" like those of physics, true whenever certain circumstances are present. As Leonard Bloomfield used to remark, there is no more sense in talking about "Grimm's law" than there would be in referring to "the law of Gettysburg". "Grimm's sound-change" or "Grimm's formulation" would be much better terms.

As for exceptions, of course they can be found for every sound-change, and often in large numbers, as in the passage just cited from Tolomei. However, not only were extensive sets of correlations between obviously related and not so obviously re-lated languages formulable as "laws", but closer examination re-vealed that many of the apparent exceptions could in their turn be correlated with previously unobserved phenomena. This was what Karl Verner did when he found an explanation for an ap-parent exception to Grimm's formulation, correlating the differ-ence in treatment of intervocalic consonants in Germanic with the position of the stress attested in Greek and Sanskrit and hence attributable to Proto-Indo-European. It was, or should have been, obvious that, no matter what the theoretical failings of the *Jung-grammatiker* formulation of the principle, its usefulness and, indeed, its indispensability, could not be denied. Later efforts—such as that of M. G. Bàrtoli in his "Neolinguistica", with its geographical "norms" or rules-of-thumb—to replace it have proven unsuccessful, and the assumption of regularity in sound-change still remains essential in historical linguistics.

We need to look farther than the old and by now out-worn debate between Neo-Grammarians and their opponents, so as to see what is really at the base of this assumption and its fruit-

[117]

fulness. One of the major difficulties on both sides was that they did not clearly understand that they were dealing, not with a statement of fact, but with an assumption concerning how phenomena WOULD behave if there were no interference: in this case, that phonemes change, and would change regularly if not interfered with by other factors. This is a scientific postulate of the same type as Newton's "laws" of physics: that an object at rest would remain at rest if not moved by some force; that an object in motion would continue moving in a straight line if not deflected therefrom by some force; etc.[1] Whether the conditions specified in such an assumption are ever verified in observed situations, is beside the point: the assumption is what enables us to plot an expected development (e.g. the course that an object would take, or the regular out-come of any given phoneme or cluster), and to measure the observed phenomena against what might be expected, so as to find clues to the cause of the deviation.

Hypotheses set up to explain any given deviation may turn out to be valid, or they may not; but the untenability of any specific explanation offered under the assumption of regular phonemic change does not render the assumption itself invalid. Thus, the deviant development of Proto-Romance /p t k/ to /b d g/ in some Italian words (e.g. *strada* "way" > PRom. /stráta/, *luogo* "place" > PRom. /lóku/) was explained by Meyer-Lübke as due to differences in the place of word-stress, similarly to Verner's formulation for Germanic consonants. This explanation is no longer considered valid by most scholars, because it assumed too many inexplicable exceptions; at present, some kind of bor-

1. It has been objected that Newton's laws of physics have been superseded by the principle of relatively, as propounded by Einstein, and that hence our parallel is not valid. However, Newtonian physics is still valid for our world and for the solar system; similarly, although we can imagine non-human behavior for which our postulate of regular sound-change would not hold, it does retain its validity for humans as they are at present constituted (and will continue to be in any foreseeable future).

[118]

rowing (from regional or social dialects, or both) is a more satisfactory explanation for this divergent development. However,
both types of explanation are equally acceptable under the assumption of regular phonemic change; we cannot do as Bàrtoli
did, calling the first "typically Neo-Grammarian" and the second
"typically Neo-Linguist".

The cause of the regularity observed in sound-change is to
be sought in the habitual nature of human articulatory behavior.
Phonemes are units of sound which is produced habitually and
hence normally outside of the speaker's awareness. When habits
change, they do so in a regular fashion, like-wise outside of awareness. The mechanism of sound-change is a gradual shift in allophonic variation, a progressive favoring of one sound-type over
another. The nineteenth-century theoreticians of sound-change
were therefore justified in distinguishing *schleichender Laut-
wandel* or gradual sound-change from the sudden type, or
springender Lautwechsel. This latter involves, not a gradual shift
in articulatory aims, but the instant replacement of one phoneme
by another, for any one of various reasons. Chief among these is
borrowing of one kind or another, either internal, by analogy (as
in the case of Old French *lievet* ≠ Modern French *lève*, p. 114),
or external, from a related form in some other dialect or language—as when a speaker who says *clim* for the past of *climb* in
one dialect of English hears and takes over the form *clum* from
another.

Another source for sudden replacement is the generalization
of one of the unsystematic changes that are always going on, as
nonce-events, on the fringes of any speaker's idiolectal system.
Each one of us is always making slips of one kind or another, involving metathesis, as in *irrevelant* for *irrelevant;* dissimilation,
e.g. *silted* for *stilted;* haplology, as in *the atly* for *the atlas of Italy;*
and similar irregularities. When a speaker makes such a slip repeatedly, either through inattention or deliberately (as when he
is trying to be funny), it may become generalized and pass over
into his habitual behavior. From one speaker, it can spread to

[119]

others, and eventually become part of the community's usage. Childish mispronunciations are often taken up in this way, becoming part of a family's dialect (such as one child's /múwgis/ for *music*, and another's /sǽmbəl/ for *sandal*), or even part of the regular usage of a whole speech-community (e.g. *tummy* for *stomach*). Many of our nick-names come, as is well known, from this source, for instance *Meg* or *Peg* for *Margaret*, *Molly* for *Mary*. But the main part of each speaker's phonological repertory is the systematic core of his pronunciation-habits; it is this latter which is involved in regular sound-change.

To avoid the confusion resulting from the needless name-calling that took place in the debate over the Neo-Grammarians and "phonetic law", it is desirable to replace the old terminology with a new one, which (we may hope) can remain free of polemic associations. As we have seen (p. 117), historical linguistics rests on the assumption that phonemes change, and would change regularly if not interfered with.[2] All scholars who have done successful work in historical linguistics have, overtly or tacitly, based their studies on this assumption. We may, therefore, use the term "regularist" for any-one who adopts the postulate of regular sound-change in his work, and distinguish at least three types of regularists:

A. Any-one, at any time (from Claudio Tolomei onward) who
   has worked on this principle;
B. Brugmann, Leskien, and their followers in the 1870's:
   these, and these only, we will call Neo-Grammarians;
C. Those who use the regularist postulate in their work, but
   deny it overtly; these may best be termed "crypto-regu-
   larists".

As opposed to these, we may apply the term "sporadicists" to scholars who deny the validity of the regularist postulate in

2. Regularity in sound-change, as an assumption, must not be confused with the (often rather artificial) rigidity with which many uninspired and uninspiring manuals of historical phonology present their data.

theory and who do not adopt it in their work. Of these, there are only a few left, and they are found mainly in the ranks of the amateurs who, following in the foot-steps of N. Ja. Marr, try to derive all words in all the world's languages from a few basic root-syllables, or to establish a close relationship between (say) Germanic and Algonquian. Without structural analysis in terms of emic units and their relations, descriptive linguistics could not be scientific; without the regularist postulate, historical linguistics could not be scientific either.

Closely tied in with the postulate of regular sound-change is the validity of the comparative method and of the reconstruction of proto-languages. There are many groups or "families" of languages which show structural resemblances too great to be due to chance, or yet to extensive borrowing from some other language, and which must clearly have developed by differentiation from a common source. The common source of such a group can be reconstructed, at least in part (depending on the extent of the data available), on the basis of the evidence of the later stages, if systematic correspondences are present throughout in phonology, morphology, syntax, and lexicon. That this procedure is valid, is shown by the case of reconstructed Proto-Romance, which is close enough to (though not identical with) attested Latin to show that we can make a realistic approximation to the basic structure out of which the Romance languages developed.[3] The definitive proof of the validity of comparative reconstruction was given by Leonard Bloomfield in the Algonquian field, by his discovery of a Swampy Cree form /mihtkusiw/ "he is red", with a special consonant-cluster /htk/ occurring only in this morpheme

3. The terms *genetic relationship, family, mother-languages, daughter-languages,* etc., often used in comparative linguistics, have quite misleading implications if taken literally, since languages are not organisms and do not reproduce either sexually or asexually. However, these terms are so widely used that it would be difficult to persuade scholars to replace them; perhaps we can continue using them, provided we forget all biological or zoölogical over-tones in their meaning.

[121]

and corresponding exactly with a special consonant-cluster */çk/ which Bloomfield had set up for Proto-Central-Algonquian on the basis of a discrepant correspondence in this particular morpheme in other Algonquian languages. Curiously enough, he demonstrated this just at a time when many scholars in the Indo-European field were doubting the validity of the comparative method. But the comparative method, tested and proven in such widely diverse fields as Romance, Germanic, Indo-European, Finno-Ugric, Semitic, and Algonquian, depends for its very foundation on the postulate of regular sound-change (without which no comparison at all could be made). This postulate is, as we have seen, a scientific assumption; and its use in comparative linguistics and reconstruction is, therefore, what gives this approach to language-history its scientific character and value.

8

LINGUISTICS AND OTHER DISCIPLINES

What is the place of linguistics among the various intellectual disciplines? For many hundreds of years, speculation concerning language was a part of philosophy and logic. In the nineteenth century, a widely held view placed linguistics among the natural sciences, with many points of contact between the study of language and that of biology, especially (in August Schleicher's case) with botany. In the twentieth century, there have been some interpretations of the rôle of linguistics which would place it among the social sciences, and some assigning it to the humanities. Most recently, there has been a strong movement directed towards putting linguistics back into its mediaeval function as a hand-maiden of philosophy and logic. It will, therefore, be valuable for us to pause, now that we have considered the nature of language and the methods of linguistics, and to examine the relation of linguistics to other fields of knowledge.

First, however, a brief word concerning the nature of science, and especially the much-discussed difference between the *Naturwissenschaften* or "natural sciences" and *Geisteswissenschaften* or "spiritual sciences". We saw in Chapter 1 that science, as an approach to the study of ourselves and the world in which we live, has certain fundamental characteristics: an inductive approach (starting from and remaining basically anchored to observed phenomena); procedure by hypothesis, testing, and verifi-

[123]

cation; objectivity; and tentativeness. Testing is, for some subject-matters (such as the broader aspects of human behavior), not as easily done as it is for some others. This is the main difference between the social sciences and the "hard" or laboratory-sciences; but it is not basic to the application of scientific method. The opposition between *Natur-* and *Geisteswissenschaften* is spurious, since there is no need to assume a separate, non-physical entity called "Geist" ("spirit", soul", "mind", etc.) as a necessary factor in human activity that can never be observed but to which phenomena of our behavior can be ascribed at will.[1] If we choose to deny—as did Croce and the idealists—that scientific method is applicable to the study of language at all, that is another matter, and the debate moves onto different ground. In our discussion here, however, we have assumed that the application of scientific method in linguistics is both feasible and desirable. If it is, the approach to be followed will be that out-lined above; the methods of science are the same, no matter what subject-matter they are applied to. There is no difference between *Natur-* and *Geisteswissenschaft;* there is only *Wissenschaft,* science.

Insofar as its subject-matter is a type of group-behavior of humans living together, linguistics belongs in the broad classification of the social sciences, and more specifically under anthropology, the study of man-kind. Its relation to the humanities depends on the definition we give of this latter. According to some, humanistic studies deal only with manifestations of individuality—differences between one individual's doings and those of others—and particularly with features which characterize out-standing individuals and their performances in artistic endeavor (art, music,

1. It should not be, but apparently it is necessary to add that these considerations concerning the assumption of "mental" factors in scientific research and discourse have no bearing on the individual religious faith or philosophical out-look of the investigator. Christians of various persuasions, Jews, Muslims, Buddhists, and atheists all follow the same method in their work in physics, chemistry, geology, astronomy, etc.; a truly objective, scientific approach should enable the same common habits of work and findings to prevail in the social sciences, including linguistics.

and, most important for the linguist, literature). Viewed from this angle, the humanities have little or nothing in common with the social sciences, and many humanists even view these latter as inimical to the understanding and appreciation of works of art. Others, however—myself included—consider this breach between the humanities and the social sciences as unfortunate, another manifestation of that split into "two cultures" which Sir Charles P. Snow has rightly lamented. From a broader point of view, the contrast between individual and society is largely illusory: the only way that humans exist is as individuals, but they have to exist in groups—always at least two (mother and child), but normally many more together in a socially organized context. Hence the study of everything individual is also part of that of man-kind as a whole, and the humanities are a branch of anthropology, more specifically of cultural anthropology.

Linguistics has ties with various branches of anthropology, especially physical and cultural; less with archaeology. This latter is relevant to linguistics insofar as it involves the discovery and dating, by non-linguistic criteria, of attestations of earlier speech (especially inscriptions). In the absence of directly interpretable data, further correlations between presumed linguistic history and archaeological finds are at best tenuous and unsure, and at worst misleading, as when efforts are made to interpret certain types of dwellings (e.g. the terramara culture of northern Italy) as relics of a certain stage of Indo-European or Italic migration. Physical anthropology is relevant because we use the respiratory system, from the diaphragm up, for speaking; the auditory system for hearing; and the brain for decoding what we hear and encoding what we say. To date, what physical anthropology has had to tell us about differences in language-capacity between races and sub-races is almost wholly negative: that, at the present stage of human development, all normal people's physical equipment for speaking is the same, and that hence we must look elsewhere for explanation of the differences we find between languages. Negative information, however, is just as valuable as positive, in

[125]

that it saves us from wasting time on fruitless search for non-existent correlations.

The ties of linguistics with cultural anthropology are greater, on the whole, than with other branches, simply because the object of our study is one kind of cultural activity. It is an activity of humans which is determined neither by heredity nor by the physical environment, and which each individual learns (by imitating others) as he grows up, and transmits to others (by serving as a model for imitation) in his turn. The methods used by linguists in obtaining their data are essentially the same, in their over-all pattern, as those of cultural anthropologists: observing people's actions either directly or by asking them what they do, and analyzing documentation of behavior not observable by direct examination or elicitation. (This latter type of analysis is inevitable, of course, in our study of past behavior, especially in historical studies.)

On the other hand, linguistic structure is exceptionally self-contained, as compared with other types of cultural activity, so that it can be formulated, if necessary, largely without reference to the rest of the culture of which it is a part. If the linguistic analyst takes too formalistic (pseudo-mathematical or -logical) an attitude towards his material, and tries on this account to neglect considerations of meaning in his analysis, he may tend to pay too little attention to the fact that a linguistic structure is, especially because of the meanings inseparable from it, part of its speakers' culture. By now, almost all scholars working in the field of modern prestige-cultures normally learn their target-languages well enough to spend at least some time in the societies whose culture and literature they study, and thus to act as "participant-observers". Unfortunately, linguists who work on non-prestigious dialects or aboriginal tongues do not learn them this well, and their accounts of such languages suffer as a result. (A notable exception was Leonard Bloomfield, who became, it is said, a fluent speaker of Menomini.)

In recent years, considerable attention has been paid to the interrelations between language and social structure, in the inter-disciplinary field of socio-linguistics. Here, attention has been concentrated primarily on the implications of speakers' choices, among options available to them in their linguistic patterns, for their standing in the community and their relation to one group or another. As long as scholars were concerned almost exclusively with a single, supposedly absolutely unified 'standard language and with works of artistic merit written therein, it was possible to set up a simple dichotomy between "good" and "bad" (or "correct" and "incorrect", "well-formed" and "ill-formed", or what have you), and to dismiss from consideration all phenomena which did not fall under the first of the two headings in each of these dichotomies. Now that scholars no longer base their work on such narrow, exclusive criteria, we have become aware of extensive variation along a scale ranging from pedantically over-correct all the way to many types of non-standard usage—for *library*, for instance, from /lájbərèrij/ to /lájbrèrij/ to /lájbrij/ to /lájbèrij/. Each choice, in instances of variation like this, tells hearers something about the status of the speaker—often with different over-tones for different hearers.[2] Techniques of fine-grained phonetics and phonemics, structural description, semantics, and dialect-geography join with sociological analysis in discovering correlations between linguistic and social structure, for practical as well as theoretical purposes.

Another extensively developed interdisciplinary field has been psycholinguistics, with approximately similar aims—the

2. As in the situation reported for *ain't* in Charleston, S.C.: both upper- and lower-class speakers are quite secure in using this form, and if some-one carefully avoids it, this is evidence that he is afraid that those who hear him saying *ain't* will think that he came from up-country and that his grand-pappy went around bare-foot—which is probably true! A rather Pirandellian situation arises in cases like these, where not only the speaker's view of his own behavior is involved, but also others' view of it, his idea of what others think of him, their idea of what he thinks they think . . . and so forth.

[127]

establishment of correlations between linguistic phenomena and the findings of psychology. Here, the situation is somewhat more ticklish than in socio-linguistics, because the field of psychology itself is (and has been for a long time) in a state of extensive up-heaval, and great confusion has recently been re-introduced into linguistics. There is at present no discoverable consensus among psychologists over the relevance or even existence of "mental" factors in humans' make-up, or over the acceptability of results obtained through techniques of introspection or other non-objec-tive procedures of observation. The feud between behaviorists and subjectivists is as strong as ever. Psycholinguists, therefore, is open to as many interpretations as its practitioners espouse faiths in psychology and linguistics. In the nineteenth century, psychol-ogy had a hard fight to establish its independence from philos-ophy; in the twentieth, linguistics had a similar struggle to free itself from the dominance of any one school of psychology. For the first half of the century, each successive step in freeing linguistics from psychological preconceptions was accompanied by a corresponding advance in scientific technique in our study of language. Current efforts to re-subject linguistic theory to one particular brand of psychology (mentalist, subjectivist) have already resulted in long slides backward and downward; they must be halted if linguistics is to retain its independence as an intellectual discipline. Until this is done, psycholinguistics will re-main suspect, to be approached with caution, and its findings can be accepted only tentatively.

The same considerations hold, even more strongly, for the relations of linguistics with philosophy. As long as concern with language was a province of philosophers and logicians—all through the Middle Ages, that is, and largely continuing into the Renaissance and early modern times—no scientific linguistics was possible. To attain a scientific approach to language, it was neces-sary (and it took several centuries in the doing) to discard aprioristically imposed categories of logic—"modes of existence and signification" and the like. Linguistic structure is not determined by logic and does not express logical categories, but goes far beyond them, in both its range and its adaptability to use in real-life situations. Uncritical philosophers—such as the Platonists and the mediaeval "Modistae"—are likely to substitute the categories of some grammatical structure for classifications derived from actual experience and experiment (and then, mistaking their grammatically-derived categories for pre-existing "ideal" modes of thought, turn around and criticise the very grammarians from whose work they have unreflectingly derived them). If, to empty mediaeval speculations, there is added the absolutism and authoritarianism of a dictatorial *Weltanschauung*, such as that of seventeenth-century France, we have the tyranny of an absolute linguistic standard backed up by the pseudo-logic of such a grammar as the *Grammaire de Port-Royal* of Arnauld and Lancelot (1660), pretending to establish universally valid principles for the structure of all languages, but in actuality basing them on that of only three (Latin, Greek and French). There is no room for reactionary philosophical or logical speculations in linguistics, and recent efforts to re-introduce them are threatening to negate all the progress achieved over four centuries (since the time of Claudio Tolomei), dragging our understanding of language back down to a state of mediaeval ignorance and obscurantism.

With history, linguistics has obvious connections, principally because our written documentations of earlier stages of any given language are by no means complete in themselves, and need interpretation in the light of all other available knowledge. Texts like the Oaths of Strassburg (842), for instance, benefit from the detailed study of the situation in which they were uttered. From a longer-range point of view, like-wise, it is essential to have as clear a picture as possible of the situation accompanying, say, the differentiation of Latin in late Imperial times and during the break-up of the Roman Empire. Without such knowledge, we are likely to make blunders in interpretation—as when it was thought that the Oaths of Strassburg must be heavily Latinized in their

[129]

form, just because they occur in the middle of a Latin historical text and may have been prepared by a Latin-speaking scholar. The relation between linguistics and history is bilateral, each on occasion aiding the other. For instance, it used to be thought that, during the period of Moslem rule in Spain, the entire population must have spoken Arabic, and that no Romance speech had survived at all. Our view of the whole situation was radically altered when attestations of very archaic Ibero-Romance ("Mozarabic") were found in the refrains of Arabic and Hebrew poems (the ḫarǧas), showing that part of the population did speak Romance all through the period. This discovery has, in its turn, altered our view of the relations between Moors and Christians in Moslem Spain, making it evident that they were much more complicated than was previously thought. On the other hand, caution is also necessary, especially in trying to establish presumed historical events (e.g. migrations) on the basis of purely linguistic relationships (cf. p. 125).

In the humanities, linguistics has the closest relationship with the study of literature, as might be expected from the fact that this latter has language as the artistic medium in which it is cast. The two fields are blended in philology, the interpretation of earlier texts in the light of the culture out of which they arose and the qualities imparted to them by their writers' use of the linguistic medium. In the nineteenth century, linguistic and literary analysis were, in the best scholars' work, happily blended, with neither one predominating over the other. More recently, with the development of divergent, often mutually hostile attitudes and approaches (especially Crocean and Vosslerian idealism in work on literature, and a scientific aim in linguistics), the unity of philology has been broken. It can be restored only by a renewed understanding of how both literature and language are related to life and to the culture of which both are a part.

Literature itself needs to be defined rather more broadly than has often been done in our narrow humanistic tradition. One broad definition, which takes into account the social function of literature as well as its aesthetic and moral values, is as "any discourse, short or long, on which some of the members of a community set positive value, and which they insist on having repeated from time to time in essentially unchanged form" (cf. p. 47). The great masterpieces of our world literatures fit comfortably into this definition (each time we read Dante or Shakespeare, we are having him repeated for us), and so do other works—ranging from somewhat-less-than-great all the way down to "kitsch"—by which at least some members of our community set store, even if high-brow literary critics do not. This definition also has the merit of covering oral as well as written literature. Its wording is general enough so as to include literary values as part of the criterion, but at the same time it avoids identifying these values specifically. After all, literary and aesthetic values are notoriously varied and shifting in time, space, and culture.

Looked at from this point of view, literature is seen to have a somewhat different function in society from that which many people assign to it. It is part of culture, but it is not necessarily the highest expression of culture. It is not a full or a balanced reflection of culture—inevitably not, since all art involves a selection of features to be emphasized and an omission of others considered unessential—and hence is not the measure of culture. We can often learn more about a culture from mediocre literature, or even from pure "bilge", than from greater, but less representative works. In its relation to the public, literature occupies an important place, in that it is the repository of much of the culture's traditions when these are lost, the bearers of the culture become, as has been said, "marginal men", with far less orientation to the world and to themselves than their ancestors had. Yet, important though it is, this function of literature must not be over-emphasized. If a man of letters is a leader or a prophet, it is by virtue of his message, and any literary value that his work may have is simply the aspect by which his message is made interesting or attractive. Similarly, the study of literature is, as we have seen, part of cultural anthropology. It is not (except for some of its

[131]

practitioners) the center, nor even the main concern, of intellectual life, nor is its history identical with that of ideas or culture.

In its relation to language, literature obviously depends for its artistic qualities on the structural features of the language in which it is composed. Since languages differ so widely in their grammatical structures and their lexica, and in the semantic correlations of both of these, the literatures based thereon must also differ widely. Everything can be said in every language, albeit often with a considerable amount of paraphrase; but there will be certain things that some languages will be considerably better adapted for saying concisely with their grammatical mechanism and with their semantics, than others. Hence, although intellectual content may remain the same, the aesthetic and stylistic potentialities of languages will differ enormously. As Edward Sapir said:

> Style is not an absolute, a something that is to be imposed
> on the language from Greek or Latin models, but merely
> the language itself, running in its natural grooves, and with
> enough of an individual accent to allow the artist's personality
> to be felt as a presence, not as an acrobat.

Hence we can find such qualities, deriving from the nature of the language, as elaborately periodic structure in Latin and Greek, compactness and terseness in Chinese, smoothness in French,[3] and loose, free, almost rambling style in English.

These effects on the aesthetics of literary style are derived from all levels of linguistic structure. The presence of nasal vowels in French makes it possible—as many poets have found, and as Stéphane Mallarmé stated explicitly and rightly—to obtain effects which are not possible in languages lacking nasal vowels. It is the absence of phonemic stress in French, and the almost

---

3. But not "logicality"; French is neither more nor less logical than any other language. (p. 42).

[132]

even flow of syllables in the breath-group, that gives French the distinctive quality to which Sainte-Beuve was referring in his famous remark about Racine, "Il rase la prose, mais avec des ailes." Latin inflectional complexity, syntactic freedom, and semantic range enabled Roman authors to make lapidary statements, saying a great deal in a very few words, and often with extensive connotative overtones, as in Vergil's *Sunt lachrymae rerum, et mentem mortalia tangunt.*

It follows that the study of the characteristics of each literature depends, much more than is often overtly realized, upon a knowledge of the features of linguistic structure which make these characteristics possible. To a large extent, and in a somewhat unsystematic fashion, critics and historians of literature have indeed taken linguistic factors into account, but depending for the most part on not wholly satisfactory traditional formulations of grammar. Much has been done recently, and far more still remains to be done, in analyzing the way in which authors have utilized the potentialities of their linguistic structure. This is an excellent path to pursue, provided we realize that in such study no value-judgments are to be made in either direction. A literature is not good or bad because of any qualities inherent in the language used as its medium. Contrariwise, a language is not more meritorious or worthy of study just because it has had great literature written in it. To quote Sapir again:

> Language is itself the collective art of expression, a summary of thousands upon thousands of individual intuitions.[4] . . . The language is ready, or can quickly be made ready, to define the artist's individuality. If no literary artist appears, it is not essentially because the language is too weak an instrument, it is because the culture of the people is not favorable to the growth of such personality as seeks a truly individual verbal expression.

4. My own re-phrasing of this would be "a summary of countless millions of individuals' experiences".

[133]

With music, language shares certain basic features of design, particularly the use of successive but different pitches, with possible variations in length, intensity, and timbre. Both convey "meanings", and thereby influence their listeners. Beyond this point, however, the differences between them are greater than the similarities. On the one hand, language goes far beyond music in the objectivity and relative exactitude of its correlations with the world around us. Music conveys only connotative meanings, associated with emotions which are always vague and indefinable. In language, both contentives and functors (including syntactic features) have denotational meanings that can be defined with a certain amount of exactitude, at least to the extent that they are normally summarized in dictionaries and serve for our real-life use. Music makes up for its deficiencies in this respect by going far beyond language in the range to which possible variations in pitch, intensity (loudness and stress), rhythm, and length can be exploited. In these respects, the complexity of our modern orchestral and choral music is—well, hardly infinite, but far greater than anything found in the fairly simple prosodic system which the native speaker of any language learns and uses daily all his life.

There is a great deal to be done in the investigation of the relation between linguistic and musical structure. Earlier attempts (such as that of Rameau) to read a specific meaning, even if only of a connotative kind, into each pitch-relationship have been discarded. Nevertheless, we might expect that there would be a certain correlation between the musical characteristics of a community's common melodic and harmonic practice, and their linguistic structure, in its prosodic patterns (especially intonation) and basis of articulation. This is often reflected in popular music (e.g. German folk-song or American gospel hymns and rock-and-roll). The European "common practice" of the last three centuries is based largely on Italian prosodic features and basis of articulation, dating from the seventeenth century, when music and the *commedia dell'arte* were the chief exportations of

[134]

an otherwise impoverished and down-trodden Italy. In more modern times, some have seen in the musical style of certain composers, popular only in their own countries, such as Elgar in England and Fauré in France, the reflection of their native languages (British English and French, respectively, in these two instances). Whether these and similar hypotheses are valid is a question that needs further testing, which should be undertaken by scholars with thorough training in both linguistic and musical analysis.

Going in the "opposite direction", towards the natural sciences, we find considerably less relationship with linguistics. Nineteenth-century parallels between languages and biological organisms have been shown to be quite invalid. Human social groups are, as we have seen, not organisms; they are collections of individuals, beyond whom nothing "super-organic" exists. Languages, likewise, are not organisms; they are sets of habits and dispositions. They do not reproduce, either sexually or asexually. Such expressions as "mother-language", "daughter-language", and "genetic relationship among languages" are only metaphors, which we take literally only at our peril. No biological "model" can do anything but stand in the way of our understanding the real nature of language. With biology, our chief point of contact is through human physiology, since the linguist must know the parts of the body involved in encoding and decoding the message, speaking, and hearing. With biochemistry and chemistry proper, linguistics has no direct connection: we need to know that the cells of the body, and the molecules of the air through which the sound-waves pass, exist, but we do not need to know the details of their cellular or molecular structure.

Through physical anthropology, there is a certain relation between linguistics and human physiology. Here, again, the details of such matters as the type of tissue (muscular, cartilaginous, etc.) involved in the motions of the lips, tongue, or larynx, or the mechanism whereby the ear perceives sounds, are basically marginal to linguistics. They are indeed important for certain aspects

[135]

of applied linguistics, particularly speech-correction. We must know what is involved in cases of dysfunction, so as to take the proper measures, e.g. in the teaching of deaf-mutes or in helping persons who have innate or acquired defects in the speech-organs. Studies of aphasia are important, as far as they go, in casting at least an indirect light on processes of normal speech, by comparison with what can go wrong. Such information, when it is eventually obtained in more detail, should serve to re-inforce the ties between linguistics, physiology, and psychology.

There is a somewhat more direct relation between linguistics and physics, in the analysis of sound-waves and their properties. At one time, it seemed as if acoustic phonetics—especially with the help of such machines as the sound-spectrograph—were going to revolutionize linguistics by affording new insights into the nature of speech-sounds and our perception thereof. It turned out, however, that the findings of acoustic phonetics correlated quite well with what was already known on the basis of articulatory analysis, and forced no radical re-orientation in phonology. The substitution of impressionistic acoustically-based terms ("acute", "grave", "compact", "diffuse", etc.) for those based on the physiology of the speech-organs has brought no improvement in our knowledge or understanding or the phenomena themselves. Electronic physics can be of indirect assistance to the linguist in the development and handling of sound-recording-techniques. The methods used in chemical and physical experimentation are of little use to linguistics, simply because of the different nature of the subject-matter. In the human use of language, there is not much that can be subjected to even relatively short-term, completely controlled experiment. There are too many variables involved in the objective facts of human activity, and many of our doings last (or their effects last) over too long a time—to say nothing of ethical preconceptions against experimentation which might affect adversely the lives or relationships of members of society.

[136]

There has been much debate over the connection between linguistics and mathematics. At one extreme, we find those who consider linguistics practically a branch of mathematics, and who attempt to formalize the structure of language in algebraic terms. At the other are those who deny the relevance of any kind of mathematics to linguistic analysis. These two hostile view-points are only partially correlatable with the opposition between scientists and humanists. By no means all of the former subscribe to the theory that a field of study is scientific only insofar as it is mathematizable; and by no means all of the latter would deny the possibility of applying at least some types of mathematics to certain aspects of cultural and artistic manifestations. Before we can say anything about the relationships of linguistics to mathematics, however, we must look at the nature of this latter, especially with respect to language itself. Is mathematics, as a form of discourse, essentially different from and superior to language? Or is it simply a specialized development of our every-day language-behavior, differing from this latter only in certain non-essential respects?

Our answer must clearly be the latter. In its essence, mathematics is a derivative of normal language, but specialized in certain directions. Real ("natural", "ordinary", "every-day") linguistic systems have certain properties which render them highly useful in the business of normal human living. They have non-logical, uneven, irregular phonological and morpho-syntactical structures. Their semantic associations are with real-life phenomena, but not so rigorously defined as to prevent over-lapping and as to cause spur-of-the-moment difficulties or impossibilities of classification and reference in communication. In certain types of discourse, however, it is desirable to eliminate irregularities, and to extend one's reference as broadly as possible in order to cover all phenomena having certain features in common. ("Let x be a . . . . having . . . .") This is what mathematics aims to do so that its users can make increasingly less specific statements about more and more related phenomena, in a wholly regular manner. This is why "language-nuts", people who learn foreign languages easily and enjoy the process, are often hostile to mathematics: they miss both the irregularity and the specificity of real language-structure. For the purposes of mathematicians, however, it is completely justifiable to establish a limited technique of discourse, with its own special structural characteristics, as we have just described.

The trouble arises when these special characteristics are thought to be extendable and desirable either in all human use of language, or in our study thereof. Ever since ancient times, logicians and mathematicians have thought that they could re-structure normal human language to make it conform to their philosophical preconceptions (a task even more impossible than that of the legendary King Canute in rolling back the waves). Failing that aim, they have thought to construct artificial models, with which real language could be compared and against which it could be evaluated. Mathematical models have been worked out in considerable detail, and the facts of human linguistic activity have been forced into the Procrustean bed of these models, under the pretence of achieving greater "power", i.e. a level of abstraction farther removed from reality, than can be attained by other approaches. But the purpose of linguistic study is not to make abstractions *a priori;* it is to find out the actual facts first of all (and we are far from having achieved this aim completely, in any branch of linguistics), and then to make generalizations through setting up abstractions based on the facts we have observed, not by setting up models in advance and then forcing the facts into them. Since mathematics itself is only a derivative and reduction of language, it can hardly serve as a frame-work within which the greater structure, from which it is derived, can be described or evaluated.

There are, nevertheless, certain respects in which mathematics can be helpful in the study of language. Every time a speaker opens his mouth to say something, or sits down to write something, he exercises a choice among the various possibilities that are open to him; and when he has chosen a certain path, his utterance is likely to proceed in accordance with further choices that are open, and avoiding other paths that are—if he follows his normal patterns—no longer open within the frame-work of the utterance on which he has embarked. Whether he actually does so or not, however, is not wholly predictable, because there exists also the chance that he may suddenly shift from one pattern to another "in mid-stream", as it were—and we all do this, far more frequently than is usually realized. If he listens or reads, there is of course a large element of chance as to what he will be exposed to, and also a large element of predictability. In order to deal with situations in which choice and chance are involved, there is a branch of mathematics called statistics, which is eminently qualified to be applied to language as well as to many other aspects of human activity. The predictability of occurrences in any given speech-community, on the phonological, morpho-syntactical, and lexical levels, can be studied statistically, and the characteristics both of a group's behavior and that of individuals can be determined accurately enough so that, for instance, the authorship of anonymous works (e.g. the "Junius" letters) can be determined by their writers' choice of vocabulary and stylistic features. In those aspects of our language-activity which are governed by choice and chance, mathematics, in the shape of statistics, can be quite useful. Nevertheless, the rôle of mathematics remains ancillary, especially in that it can be applied only after the structure of the language and its meanings have been discovered and formulated by non-mathematical techniques.

Even though it is a branch of anthropology (in the broad sense) and hence of the social sciences; even though it is also closely related to the humanities, which are also part of cultural anthropology; even though it has connections with the natural sciences, because the human body and its physical environment are involved in the act of speech—nevertheless linguistics must remain independent of sister sciences in its approaches and methods of investigation, analysis, and formulation. That it can

[139]

do so is, as we have seen, in large measure due to the fact that language itself is a relatively free-standing aspect of our activity as humans. Each attempt to bring linguistics under the aegis of some other branch of science (biology, physics, mathematics) or of some non-scientific study (literature, philosophy) has led to neglect of crucial aspects of the nature of language. To be completely balanced in its approach, to do justice to all facets of its object of study, linguistics must remain in touch with all other studies with which it has connections through the nature of its subject-matter, but must never be subordinated to any of them.

9

THE FUNCTION OF LINGUISTICS

Our study of any given field of knowledge has to have some function in human life and society, to raise it above the level of a hobby suitable only for individual amusement and relaxation. Linguistics has major contributions to make, both to "pure" knowledge and to the application thereof to real-life situations and problems requiring a solution that only a knowledge of language and its nature can give.

In "pure" knowledge, the prime task of linguistics is to clarify, as much as possible, the nature of communication, especially among human beings. In order to do this, however, we must have some Archimedic stand-point outside of purely human activity, so as to see what is specifically human in language and what is not. (One cannot discover the basic characteristics of any phenomenon without contrasting it with others that share some, but not all, of its features.) To do this, it is not enough to sit in one's study and engage in *a priori* speculations about what "it stands to reason" that human speech must be in order to serve as a vehicle for logical ratiocination. We must look at the actual activities of humans and non-humans, and contrast them. This has already been done to a certain extent, in the rapidly expanding field of zoösemiotics. It is now possible to identify a certain number of basic design-features of human language, most of which it shares with various non-human communication-systems, but which are found *in toto* only in our own linguistic behavior. Among these are duality, productivity, arbitrariness, interchange-ability, specialization, displacement, redundancy, and cultural transmission.

Each one of these and similar features makes possible certain characteristics of our use of language. For instance, duality enables us to use a small number of phonemic "building-blocks", meaningless in themselves, to make a much larger number of meaningful combinations. From productivity derives our ability to analogize, in our use of already existing patterns of combining linguistic material, to bring forth novel utterances. Arbitrariness enables us to go far beyond the image-bound limitation inherent in iconic representation; interchangeability makes it possible for each normal person to act as both sender and receiver of messages. By virtue of specialization, language serves only its own goal, that of sending and receiving messages, without becoming confused with other types of activity. Displacement makes it possible for humans to talk about things which are not present in the immediate environment (and, together with negation, to make false but uncheckable statements, i.e. to tell lies). If language were not redundant, it could not be used in situations where there was considerable interference with the sending or receiving of messages (e.g. when the speaker is out of breath, or there is a great amount of back-ground-noise). Since language is transmitted culturally, there is no practical limit on the kind or amount of information that can be handed down from one individual or one generation to the next, and as a result human knowledge can be made cumulative in a way that is seemingly impossible for other species.

To what extent do humans know their environment, and of what nature is their environment? This question has been asked by philosophers for thousands of years, in their discussions of epistemology, and has been answered in different ways, many of them involving abstract speculation concerning the nature of cognition. In general, linguistic analysts have complained that traditional philosophy does not take enough account of the rôle of language in cognition. Some linguists have even gone so far as to say that language is paramount, at least implying that other factors have little or no importance. This would certainly be an exaggeration. Many things go on inside our heads without language being involved. Among non-linguistic factors in cognition are, of course, the messages which our senses bring us, and which are our fundamental source for the data which we have concerning the world and on which our brains operate. (The old doctrine of "innate ideas" has long since been abandoned by any philosopher or scientist who expects to be taken seriously.) Beyond the data afforded us by our senses, we certainly have—apparently as part of our genetic inheritance—the ability to perceive features which diverse phenomena have in common; to set up classes on the basis of these features; to use symbols; and to establish correlations between symbols and classes of phenomena, i.e. to give meanings to symbols.

Beyond this point, language steps in, and has the effect primarily of affording pre-fabricated categories of form and meaning which we learn as part of our linguistic systems, when we build these latter in ourselves by imitating them from others in our speech-community. Into these categories we fit, when sending messages to each other and to ourselves,[1] our symbolization of our perceptions of phenomena and their relation to each other and to us. No single linguistic system has enough structural categories and associated meanings (e.g. tense, mood, aspect) to afford complete symbolization for every experience we have and every relationship we perceive. This means that whatever categories are included in the system of any given speaker's idiolect are inevitably selective. By using these particular cate-

1. Most "thinking" involves formulation by means of inner speech, i.e. talking to ourselves, and therefore a dialogue in which the thinker talks back and forth, taking the rôles of both interlocutors successively in his internal discussion.

[143]

gories of form and meaning many, many thousands of times every day in his speech (external and internal), the speaker inevitably comes to regard them as normal, and, if he knows no other linguistic structure, is inclined to mistake them for universal categories of human thought. It was this wide-spread phenomenon that lay at the base of Sapir's observation, developed farther by Whorf, that a speaker's linguistic structure constitutes, as it were, a pair of spectacles through which he views the world, and whose built-in emphases (and omissions!) inevitably affect and distort his views of it.

There has been considerable discussion of this "Sapir-Whorf hypothesis". Much of the debate has been over exaggerated, untenable forms of the hypothesis, as if, for instance, Whorf, in his use of Hopi structure to illustrate his point, had asserted that Hopi had actually caused its speakers to develop a new physics, with greater theoretical emphasis on wave-like phenomena, than we find in West European physics—whereas in actuality the Hopi developed no theoretical physics at all. To argue along these lines, however, is to miss the point—in this instance, that IF the Hopi had developed a theory of physics, the structure of their language might well have caused them to focus their attention immediately on wave-like phenomena because such phenomena are easily referred to in Hopi verb-formation. The Sapir-Whorf hypothesis is useful chiefly as a development and refinement of the observation that naïve philosophizing about the world and its structure is likely to be strongly influenced by the grammatical categories of the philosopher's native language and their meanings, unless he is aware of this danger and takes steps to avoid it. (As far back as 1880, Sayce remarked that Aristotle's "categories of predication" would have been very different had he been a native speaker of a Bantu language instead of an Indo-European one.) Sapir and Whorf's warning is especially necessary in a time of uncritical return to the doctrines of "universal grammar" *à la* Port-Royal, which in reality do nothing but project onto our view of language and of the world a false logic derived from the structure of Latin,

[144]

Greek, and French. To know our world and the environment in which we live, we must develop approaches and techniques which will enable us to grasp reality as it exists outside of ourselves and outside of all linguistic structure; this is the task of science.

Of the applications of linguistics, its use in various aspects of the educational process is the best known. Since, in learning a second language, we always come up against difficulties, of which at least some are caused by the differences between the structure of our native tongue and that of the target-language, linguistic analysis can help us to identify these differences and drill to overcome the difficulties that they cause. This has always been done by skillful language-teachers, either intuitively or with such aids as have been provided by traditional techniques of foreign-language-grammar and -drills. What linguistics affords in this connection is primarily a more systematic and thorough formulation of the structures involved, and hence a more complete view of possible points (often previously unidentified) where trouble may arise, or better understanding of why they arise (e.g. with the meanings and use of Spanish *ser* and *estar* "to be"). Needless to say, contrastive linguistics is not a universal panacea; there are other sources for language-learners' difficulties than the differences between native-language- and target-language-structure. Culturally determined attitudes (particularly inhibitions against making strange sounds in strange combinations, with strange meanings), differences between native and foreign culture, and general level of intelligence—all these can cause trouble, as well as differences in linguistic structure.

Linguistics has been able to gain a footing relatively rapidly in the foreign-language-field because of the obvious advantages deriving from its use. In native-language-teaching, the extension of linguistic knowledge has taken place at a much slower rate, especially in those countries where a grammatical tradition has been strongly entrenched for centuries or millennia. The situation is due in part to inertia, and in part to vested interests, especially

[145]

those of publishers who have put huge sums of money into series of text-book which they do not want to see driven off the market by anything else, no matter how much better it may be. By the thorough re-working of teaching-procedures and texts, it would be possible to save years of our children's schooling, and to help more of them to learn reading, spelling and grammar effectively. At the out-set of the learning-process, children are fascinated by language, and love to talk about it, play with it, and invent new languages or distortions of existing language (such as Pig-Latin). That our students lose this interest and, in many instances, come to hate grammar, is the fault of our inherited procedures of teaching them, not the truth about their language and its structure, but the old falsehoods of eighteenth- and nineteenth-century traditional grammar. When students discover how untrue their school-book-grammar is to the actual facts, they rightly turn against it; but they have nothing else to substitute for it, and by the time they discover its falsity, they have passed the optimum stage for speakers to be interested in observing their own use of language and analyzing it. The early application of the findings of linguistics would serve to keep this interest alive and profitable.

Outside of the school-room, there is a great deal which our culture can learn from linguistics with regard to attitudes towards language and its function in society. This is especially true with respect to those aspects of language concerning which our culture (like, I suspect, all cultures) has a well-established and all-pervasive folk-lore, especially concerning writing, correctness, and linguistic change. It is always the duty of linguistic scientists to get it through their fellow-citizens' heads that speech is prior to writing, from all points of view, in human language; that standards of usage, although they exist, are all relative, not absolute, and are conditioned exclusively by social factors; and that change in language is inevitable (whether any-one considers it desirable or not), resulting from the inherent instability of linguistic structure, and involves no corruption or deterioration.

In its relation with psychology, linguistics can have practical application in the analysis and treatment of cases where personality-disturbance manifests itself in the alteration of the community's customary speech-patterns. It is of course necessary to have first a valid formulation of what is normal in the community's linguistic behavior, especially in such matters as intonation- and stress-patterns. (Dialectal variation must also be taken into account: what in a given region is quite abnormal may, in another dialect, be quite ordinary and non-significant.) Only a small beginning has been made in the application of linguistics to psychotherapy; there is room for a great expansion in this field, if it is soundly based on observed data, not on aprioristic theories of linguistics or psychoanalysis.

In countries with an old-established tradition of normative grammar and prescription concerning a dominant standard language, the linguist's job has been (as suggested above) to break down rigid prejudices in favor of more flexible norms. In many recently established countries, the opposite problem has existed, that of discovering and setting up a standard form of language to serve as a national *koiné*, especially where there are many dialects (mutually comprehensible or not) or different languages in use. The prime example of this situation is India, where the Constitution recognizes fourteen national languages, and there are hundreds of other languages and dialects. The linguists of these countries, seeking to establish national norms, have on occasion reproached their European and American colleagues for what has seemed an excessively dogmatic stand against prescriptivism, and a refusal to recognize the existence or validity of any norms at all.

Such an interpretation of anti-normativism is by no means justified. No-one (not even the present writer!) has ever denied the existence of all norms, nor their (limited) usefulness in certain situations. The object of the anti-normativists' animadversions has been (and should continue to be) the delusions concerning absolute correctness that prevail among speakers of most European languages. In countries where there is no standard usage at all,

[147]

it can be desirable to set up a standard, provided it is not foisted on the public-at-large as absolute and as applying to all speakers in all situations. Standardization of language, in recently established nations faced with problems of modernization, can affect only the usage of a relatively small group of people (administrators, professionals, intellectuals), and only a relatively minor aspect of linguistic structure, particularly technical vocabulary. Linguistics can bring help to language-planners by providing accurate descriptions of the linguistic structures involved, and by aiding the non-linguist to decide, in the case of competing dialects, which one is likely to prove most widely comprehensible and most acceptable to the greatest number of speakers. However, so many non-linguistic factors enter into questions of language-policy, that we must not over-emphasize the rôle of the linguist therein. He can study and analyze the linguistic side of the situation and report on his findings, with his predictions as to what will happen if they are or are not taken into account. Whether the linguist's recommendations are heeded or not, depends basically on decisions to be made outside of his sphere; in this, the linguist is in the same (not always enviable) position as any other expert in the modern political world.

In addition to the above respects in which the linguistic analyst can help further both pure and applied science, there are certain other types of activity which he should shun, since they are harmful to both science and society. Of these, the one with the highest social prestige is aprioristic speculation—which, despite its popularity in some quarters, has exercised a baneful influence on the entire development of linguistics ever since the days of the Greek philosophers. The Aristotelian "categories of predication" and the mediaeval schoolmen's "modes of existence and of predication" stood for millennia in the way of objective examination of humans' real linguistic activity, even going so far (in the case of those connecting elements which the "Modistae" called syncategoremata) as to deny the linguistic nature of some fundamental features of language. As we have seen (p. 116),

[148]

scientifically based historical linguistics began in the sixteenth century with Claudio Tolomei; but its development was set back for more than a hundred years by the influence of the unfounded rationalistic dogmas of the Port-Royal grammar, coupled with its Latin- and French-centered grammatical doctrines. If these old, long since discredited doctrines are exhumed and put at the center of linguistics—even if they are decked out in the deceptive cellophane of pseudo-mathematical logicalism—they can do nothing but drag linguistics backward and downward, negating all the progress achieved in the last four hundred years.

On a less pretentious but equally folkloristic level, some persons who have received training in linguistics use it to write popularizations (not an evil activity in itself), but telling the general public, not what it should know about language, but what it wants to hear in the way of already wide-spread misconceptions. Many members of the public are, understandably, unhappy when they are told by linguists that their ideas on language are erroneous, and need an extensive revision to bring them in line with the facts. Popularizers of the type just mentioned cater to the injured egos of such people by reassuring them, telling them in essence that they need not divest themselves of any preconceptions in order to understand the nature of language, and pandering to their belief in correctness and in the superiority of "civilized" over "primitive" languages. There are various sub-types of this brand of cheapening popularization. The "Barmecide" or "St. Patrick" school of linguistics lists features which are not present in a language ("Japanese has no number, grammatical gender, or article"); the "Ripley" or "Believe-it-or-not" school enumerates whatever may seem odd to the reader ("Ainu has a curious duplication of the French-Celtic expression for 'eighty' ['four twenties']"). The "Bullamacow" approach describes a language by quoting examples from its vocabulary, as when we are told that although Japanese lacks grammatical gender, it "determines gender by sex"—i.e. it has separate words for "bull" and "cow", "uncle" and "aunt". In the "Old Curiosity Shop", oddments and endments of

[149]

information, miscellaneous bits of unrelated linguistic data, are heaped together in a formless mass. All of this serves to delight and impress the uncritical reader, and to bring kudos and wealth to the unscrupulous "maquereau du langage" who thus prostitutes linguistics.

If linguistics is to survive and develop as a science, it must be saved from two dangers which are currently threatening it, on the basis of the two false approaches we have just discussed. Both of them embody a reaction against scientific method in favor of older approaches to language. The first of these dangers is the recrudescence of philosophical and logical apriorism, with all its accompanying baggage of logic, innate ideas, universal grammar, and the non-existent distinction between "surface" and "deep" structure. The other danger—to which the first is in some ways contributing support—is the return of normativistic, restrictive grammar, based on doctrines of correctness and re-inforced by theories of "well-formed sentences" and their formation by means of rules. There is, as we have seen, no room in linguistics for logic, rationalism, or anything nomothetic; their re-introduction constitutes, not progress, but the negation thereof.

To bring linguistics back into the path along which it has been developing since the sixteenth century, it is not enough to proclaim the ideals of science in a hortatory manner. As in all fields of knowledge, the practitioners of linguistic science must continue to demonstrate its superiority over other approaches to language, as they have been doing, with theoretical and practical works exemplifying its application. To continue this tradition, new recruits to the field must be given thorough and effective training, which will at the same time be culturally rich enough to attract their interest and maintain their loyalty. It is not sufficient for beginners to approach linguistics with no knowledge of any linguistic structure but their own,[2] with all the erroneous notions

2. An administrator of one of our major centers for training budding linguists reported to me that three quarters of his applicants come with no experience in analyzing any language other than English.

[150]

that their culture may have concerning language, and under the delusion that all they need to learn is sets of procedures for constructing formulas and concocting rules to take a given in-put and transform it into a given out-put. Linguistics is not like those games which are advertised with the slogan "No previous experience required—any number may play". If our trainees' linguistic horizon is so narrowly restricted, they will continue to be the victims—as many of them are at present—of logicians and rule-mongers, and will emerge grievously ignorant of all but a small segment of the entire field of linguistics. We must insist that our recruits be given extensive exposure and thorough training in all branches of linguistics, descriptive and historical, from phonetics through semantics, and in such closely related fields as literature and cultural anthropology. If, and only if, this is done, we can look forward to a continuation of linguistics along the lines laid down by our predecessors from Tolomei to Bloomfield, with the cumulative development that characterizes all true science, and to the further extension of the function of linguistics as, at the same time, a branch of the social sciences and of the humanities, and a bridge between the two.

10

CONCLUSION

Language is, as we have seen, something peculiarly human. The capacity to build up in oneself and to use an idiolect (and to understand closely similar idiolects) is species-specific and, as far as we can tell at present, genetically determined—one aspect of our human ability to use symbols in general. Which linguistic structure an individual learns and uses, however, is a matter of chance, depending on the community one is born into. Each speaker's idiolect is a set of habits, highly structured in its central core but with manifold irregularities and variations all around the edges, and whose structural (emic) units have meanings, i.e. correlations with the universe in which the speaker lives. Language is not determined by logical or mathematical considerations; rather, logic and mathematics are specialized types of discourse derived from linguistic structure. Logical, mathematical, and mechanical "languages" are less adequate than real languages to deal with all the shifting, unpredictable events of the world around us, since they are both reduced in structure as compared with ordinary language, and more rigid in their organization. Our approach to the study of language must be determined by its peculiar nature: linguistic analysis can be neither overly loose (poetical, impressionistic) nor overly rigid or pseudo-mathematical.

Human linguistic behavior is, in its organization, very largely independent of the structure of the surrounding world, but at the

[153]

same time it is correlated with it through meaning. Our study of language must take cognizance of both of these characteristics, treating each linguistic structure in terms of its own organization, and also analyzing each semantic structure in terms of its segmentation of our experience of the universe. These considerations apply to the various aspects under which we may consider language—panchronic, synchronic, diachronic. Only with such a holistic, but at the same time analytical approach can linguistics both remain an independent discipline and also enter into fruitful collaboration with other branches of the scientific study of mankind.

BRIEF BIBLIOGRAPHY

This bibliography is intended to give the reader the titles of a few outstanding books in which he can follow up our discussion of method. It is divided into two parts: A. books and a few articles by authors whose viewpoint is reasonably close to that advocated in this essay; B. books by authors opposed thereto.

A

BLOOMFIELD, LEONARD. 1926. "A set of postulates for the science of language". *Language* 2.135–164.
——. 1933. *Language.* New York: Holt.
BOLINGER, DWIGHT. 1968. *Aspects of language.* New York: Harcourt, Brace, and World.
CHAO, YUEN REN. 1968. *Language and symbolic systems.* Cambridge, Eng. and New York: Cambridge University Press.
GINSBERG, MORRIS. 1921. *The psychology of society.* London: Methuen.
GLEASON, HENRY ALLAN, Jr. 1961. *An introduction to descriptive linguistics.* Revised edition. New York: Holt, Rinehart, and Winston.
GOMBOCZ, ZOLTÁN. 1931. "Nyelvhelyesség és nyelvtudomány [Correctness and Linguistics]". *Magyar Nvelv* 27.1–11.
HERDAN, GUSTAV. 1966. *The advanced theory of language as choice and chance.* Berlin and New York: Springer-Verlag.
HOCKETT, CHARLES F. 1958. *A course in modern linguistics.* New York: Macmillan.
——. 1968. *The state of the art.* The Hague: Mouton.
JESPERSEN, OTTO. 1922. *Language.* London: George Allen and Unwin.
MARTINET, ANDRÉ. 1964. *Elements of general linguistics.* London: Faber and Faber, and Chicago: University of Chicago Press.
PIKE, KENNETH L. 1967. *Language in relation to a unified theory of the structure of human behavior.* Second edition. The Hague: Mouton.

SAPIR, EDWARD. 1922. *Language*. New York: Harcourt, Brace.
STURTEVANT, EDGAR HOWARD. 1947. *An introduction to linguistic science.* New Haven: Yale University Press.
WHORF, BENJAMIN LEE. 1956. *Language, thought, and reality*. Cambridge, Mass.: M.I.T. Press.

B

CHOMSKY, NOAM. 1957. *Syntactic structures*. The Hague: Mouton.
——. 1964. *Current issues in linguistic theory.* The Hague: Mouton.
——. 1965. *Aspects of the theory of snytax*. Cambridge, Mass.: M.I.T. Press.
——. 1966. *Cartesian linguistics*. New York and London: Harper and Row.
CHOMSKY, NOAM, and MORRIS HALLE. 1968. *Sound patterns of English.* New York and London: Harper and Row.
FODOR, J., and J. KATZ (eds.). 1964. *The structure of language.* Englewood Cliffs, N.J.: Prentice-Hall.
KATZ, J., and P. POSTAL. 1964. *An integrated theory of linguistic description*. Cambridge, Mass.: M.I.T. Press.

GLOSSARY

In this short glossary are listed and explained some of the most important terms occurring in this essay, giving the senses in which they are used in our discussions. No effort has been made to render this a complete listing of all terms found in present-day linguistics, nor to give meanings other than those in which the terms are used here.

allograph: a non-significant variant of a grapheme (unit of visual shape): e.g. the two shapes of the Greek letter sigma, ς (at the end of a word) and σ (elsewhere).

allomorph: a non-significant variant of a morpheme (unit of linguistic form): e.g. the stems *uom-* (before the ending *-o* in the singular) and *uomin-* before the ending *-i* in the plural) in Italian *uomo* "man" and *uòmini* "men", respectively

allophone: a non-significant variant of a phoneme (unit of sound), e.g. the two sounds [p] (unaspirated) and [p'] (aspirated) in English *spin* and *pin*, respectively.

alloseme: a non-significant variant of a sememe (unit of meaning): e.g. the two related meanings "imaginative sequence (in literature)", represented by the morpheme /fǽntəzi/ spelled *fantasy*, and "imaginative sequence (as a psychological manifestation)", represented by the same morpheme but spelled *phantasy*.

analogy: the pattern by which novel forms or constructions are coined, based on partially similar pre-existing patterns: e.g. *bring brang brung* on the analogy of *sing sang sung.*

bound form: a form occurring only together with other forms, e.g. the suffix *-ing* (as in *singing, eating, working*).

capacity: the innate ability of a human being to develop and use a linguistic system, manifested in his idiolect.

clause: a minimum unit of utterance, either *major* (also called *favorite*: e.g. in English, SUBJECT + PREDICATE, for example *John works*; in Spanish, PREDICATE alone, for example *trabaja* "[he] works"), or *minor* (any other type of clause, e.g. English *On the table., Yes.,* or *Golly!*).

[157]

competence: the total set of linguistic abilities stored by a speaker in his idiolect.

deep structure: a construction presumed, in transformational-generative grammar, to underlie another construction: e.g. *sit with a baby* as "deep structure" of *baby-sit.*

dialect: abstraction based on features common to two or more idiolects.

duality of structure: the presence, in human language, of two types of structure, the phonological (involving a small number of phonemes, which have no meaning in themselves) and the morphological-syntactical (involving meaningful sequences of phonemes and combinations of such sequences).

emic: involving the analysis of phenomena into significant functional units.

etic: involving the analysis of phenomena as raw material, without regard to their significance or function.

free form: a form which can occur alone: e.g. *table, sit, also.*

grammar: a description of the structure of a set of linguistic patterns.

grapheme: a significant unit of visual shape: e.g. any letter of the Roman alphabet.

idiolect: the totality of linguistic patterns, *in esse* or *in posse,* in the speech-behavior of an individual.

intonation: the rise and fall in pitch during the utterance of a clause (e.g. rising, falling, rising-falling).

juncture: the way in which two units of linguistic structure (especially, but not exclusively, phonemes or morphemes) are joined, as in the difference between *an aim* and *a name.*

language: (1) the institution whereby humans communicate and interact with each other, conveying messages by means of systems of habitually used oral-auditory arbitrary symbols; (2) the linguistic usage of a larger speech-community.

lexicon: the stock of words of a language.

linguistic super-ego: an individual's notion of the way other members of his speech-community expect him to act with respect to language.

linguistics: the scientific study of human language.

literature: any discourse, short or long, which at least some members of a speech-community agree in evaluating positively, and which they insist on having repeated from time to time in substantially the same form.

loan-word: a term borrowed, through imitation, by the members of one speech-community from those of another: e.g. French *joie de vivre* in English, or English (*le*) *parking* in French.

monomorphemic: consisting of only one morpheme: e.g. *hat, sit.*

morpheme: significant unit of linguistic form (whether free or bound): e.g. *hat, go, -ing.*

morphology: (1) the study of variations in morphemes; (2) the structure of such variations in a given language.

[158]

morphophonemic: pertaining to the alternations between phonemes in variant forms of the same morpheme: e.g. the alternation of /f/ and /v/ in *wife: wives.*

morphophonemics: (1) the study of morphophonemic variation; (2) the morphophonemic variations found in a given language.

performance: the manifestation, on any specific occasion, of selected features of a speaker's linguistic competence.

philology: the study of texts with a view to interpreting them from the point of view of linguistic, literary, and cultural analysis.

phoneme: a significant unit of speech-sound.

phonemic transcription: a set of graphemes used so as to represent accurately the phonemes of a language; normally enclosed in slant lines: e.g. /kæt/ *cat.*

phonemics: (1) the study of significant units of speech-sound; (2) the structure and organization of the phonemes of a given language.

phonetic: pertaining to speech-sounds, without reference to their phonemic function or organization.

phonetic transcription: a set of graphemes used so as to represent accurately the speech-sounds of a language, whether they have phonemic significance or not; normally enclosed in square brackets: e.g. ['k'æt] *cat.*

phonetics: (1) the study of speech-sounds as such; (2) the speech-sounds of a given language.

phonology: (1) the study of the phonetics, phonemics, and all other aspects of the sounds of human speech (including supra-segmental features); (2) the structure and organization of the phonological features of a given language.

prescriptive: characteristic of an approach to language in which speakers' behavior is prescribed by an "authority", whether an individual (e.g. a grammarian or a school-teacher) or an institution (e.g. an academy).

purist: one who believes in the existence of "pure", as opposed to "impure" or "corrupt", usage in language, and normally tries to follow "pure" usage himself and/or impose it on others.

rank-shift: to shift the use of a linguistic feature from the rank or level on which it normally occurs (e.g. clause) to another rank or level (e.g. phrase, as in the use of a clause as a modifier in a phrase, such as *I saw* rank-shifted in *the man I saw*).

semantic: pertaining to meaning.

semantics: the study of meaning.

sememe: a significant unit of meaning: thus, the meaning "organ of hearing" constitutes one sememe, the meaning "the part of a cereal-plant that contains the fruit" constitutes a different sememe, and both are correlated in English with the sequence of phonemes /ijr/, which therefore represents a pair of homonymous morphemes, both spelled *ear.*

speech-community: any group of two or more persons using mutually intelligible idiolects.

[159]

stress: the degree of force with which air is expelled from the lungs in uttering a syllable.

substratum: the language or dialect of a speech-community inhabiting a given territory, whose speakers give it up and instead come to speak the language of an invading or conquering group (e.g. Etruscan, Oscan, or Umbrian *vis-à-vis* Latin in ancient Italy).

subvocalization: the incomplete utterance of speech, either pronounced *sotto voce* or inhibited on the level of the nervous system.

superstratum: the language or dialect of a group of invaders or conquerors who give it up and instead come to speak the language of the population already living in the invaded country (e.g. Frankish in relation to Latin in Gaul, or Visigothic in relation to Latin in Spain).

syllable: the stretch of speech-sound between two troughs of sonority.

supra-segmental: pertaining to features of sound (e.g. juncture, syllable-structure, stress, intonation) extending over more than one phoneme in connected speech.

surface structure: in transformational-generative grammar, the actual patterns of speech in a language (presumed to be derived, at least logically, from an underlying "deep structure" and eventually traceable back to a single syntactic "kernel").

syntax: (1) the study of meaningful sequences of morphemes, above the level of morphological organization; (2) the structure and organization of such sequences in a given language.

tactics: the patterns of morphology and syntax, taken together.

transcription: a set of graphemes used to represent the sounds or phonemes of a language.

transformational-generative grammar: (1) a set of rules whereby all the well-formed sentences of a language, and no others, can be logically derived ("generated") from a single kernel-structure (SUBJECT + PREDICATE, in that order), by operations which transform one construction into another; (2) the theory of such grammars.

universals, linguistic: structural features common to all human language.